MW00676824

SOUTHERN COOKING

pil

Publications International, Ltd.

Pictured on the front cover *(clockwise from top left):* Chorizo Hash *(page 31),* Mac & Cheesiest *(page 111),* Ginger Plum Tart *(page 156)* and Spicy Buttermilk Oven-Fried Chicken *(page 56).*

Pictured on the back cover *(top to bottom):* BBQ Baked Beans *(page 109),* Pulled Pork with Honey-Chipotle Barbecue Sauce *(page 53),* Chicken and Waffles with Sriracha Maple Syrup *(page 26)* and Blueberry Peach Cobbler *(page 158).*

ISBN: 978-1-68022-513-6

Library of Congress Control Number: 2016940990

Manufactured in China.

8 7 6 5 4 3 2 1

Microwave Cooking: Microwave ovens vary in wattage. Use the cooking times as guidelines and check for doneness before adding more time.

CONTENTS

APPETIZERS AND SNACKS

GOAT CHEESE CROSTINI WITH SWEET ONION JAM

Makes 24 crostini

- 1 tablespoon olive oil
- 2 medium yellow onions, thinly sliced
- ¾ cup dry red wine
- ¼ cup water
- 2 tablespoons packed brown sugar
- 1 tablespoon balsamic vinegar
- 1 teaspoon salt
- ¼ teaspoon black pepper
- 2 ounces soft goat cheese
- 2 ounces cream cheese, softened
- 1 teaspoon chopped fresh thyme
- 1 loaf (16 ounces) French bread, cut into 24 slices (about 1 inch thick), toasted

1. Heat oil in large skillet over medium heat. Add onions; cook and stir 10 minutes. Add wine, water, brown sugar, vinegar, salt and pepper; bring to a simmer. Reduce heat to low; cook 15 to 20 minutes or until all liquid is absorbed. (If mixture appears dry, stir in a few tablespoons of additional water.) Cool 30 minutes or cover and refrigerate until ready to use.

2. Combine goat cheese, cream cheese and 1 teaspoon thyme in small bowl until well blended.

3. Spread goat cheese mixture on each slice of bread; top with onion jam.

SHRIMP FONDUE DIP

Makes about 5 cups

1 pound medium raw shrimp, peeled and deveined

½ cup water

½ teaspoon salt, divided

2 tablespoons butter, softened

4 teaspoons Dijon mustard

6 slices thick-sliced white bread, crusts removed*

1 cup milk

2 eggs

¼ teaspoon black pepper

2 cups (8 ounces) shredded Gruyère or Swiss cheese

French bread, sliced

Thick-sliced bread is often sold as "Texas toast" in supermarket bread aisles.

SLOW COOKER DIRECTIONS

1. Coat inside of slow cooker with nonstick cooking spray. Place shrimp, water and ¼ teaspoon salt in small saucepan. Cover and cook over medium heat 3 minutes or until shrimp are pink and opaque. Drain shrimp, reserving ½ cup cooking liquid.

2. Combine butter and mustard in small bowl. Spread mixture onto thick bread slices. Cut bread into 1-inch cubes. Whisk milk, eggs, reserved ½ cup cooking liquid, remaining ¼ teaspoon salt and pepper in medium bowl.

3. Spread one third of bread cubes in bottom of slow cooker. Top with one third of shrimp. Sprinkle with one third of cheese. Repeat layers twice. Pour in egg mixture. Press down on bread mixture to absorb liquid. Line lid with two paper towels. Cover; cook on LOW 2 hours or until heated through and thickened. Serve with French bread.

HEALTHY HUMMUS

Prep Time: 15 minutes • Total Time: 15 minutes • Makes 1½ cups

INGREDIENTS

- 1 can (15.25 oz.) DEL MONTE® Lima Beans, drained
- 1 clove garlic, minced
- ¼ cup chopped sweet white onion
- 2 to 3 Tbsp. lemon juice (to taste)
- 2 Tbsp. sesame seed oil
- ¼ tsp. ground cumin
- Toasted pita bread wedges (optional)
- Fresh vegetables (optional)
- Red bell pepper, diced (optional)
- Dash cayenne (optional)

DIRECTIONS

1. Combine first 6 ingredients in blender or food processor; purée until smooth.

2. Chill or serve at room temperature with pita wedges and vegetables. Garnish with red pepper and cayenne, if desired.

BREADED GREEN BEANS

Makes 6 servings

1 egg

1 pound green beans, ends trimmed

½ cup dry bread crumbs

¼ cup grated Parmesan cheese

1 tablespoon olive oil

½ teaspoon garlic powder

¼ teaspoon salt

Ranch or other creamy salad dressing (optional)

1. Preheat oven to 425°F. Line large baking sheet with parchment paper.

2. Whisk egg in large bowl. Add green beans; toss to coat. Combine bread crumbs, Parmesan cheese, oil, garlic powder and salt in small bowl. Sprinkle over green beans; toss to coat. Spread green beans on prepared baking sheet in single layer.

3. Bake 12 minutes. Turn and bake 10 minutes or until crispy. Serve with dressing.

SAUSAGE PINWHEELS

Makes 48 pinwheels

2 cups biscuit mix

½ cup milk

¼ cup butter or margarine, melted

1 pound BOB EVANS® Original Recipe Roll Sausage

Combine biscuit mix, milk and butter in large bowl until blended. Refrigerate 30 minutes. Divide dough into two portions. Roll out one portion on floured surface to ⅛-inch-thick rectangle, about 10×7 inches. Spread with half the sausage. Roll lengthwise into long roll. Repeat with remaining dough and sausage. Place rolls in freezer until firm enough to cut easily. Preheat oven to 400°F. Cut rolls into thin slices. Place on *ungreased* baking sheets. Bake 15 minutes or until golden brown. Serve hot. Refrigerate leftovers.

NOTE: This recipe can be doubled. Refreeze after slicing. When ready to serve, thaw slices in refrigerator and bake.

SOUTHERN PIMIENTO CHEESE

Prep Time: 15 minutes • Chill Time: 30 minutes • Makes 2¼ cups spread

- 1 package (3 ounces) cream cheese, softened
- ⅓ cup HELLMANN'S® or BEST FOODS® Real Mayonnaise
- 2 cups shredded Cheddar cheese (about 8 ounces)
- ½ cup drained and chopped pimientos (about 4 ounces)
- ½ cup finely chopped green onions
- ¼ cup finely chopped pimiento-stuffed green olives
- 1 teaspoon garlic powder with parsley
- 1 teaspoon paprika

1. In medium bowl with wire whisk, beat cream cheese and HELLMANN'S® or BEST FOODS® Real Mayonnaise until smooth. Stir in remaining ingredients until blended. Chill until ready to serve.

2. Serve at room temperature and, if desired, with crackers or party-size bread.

FIESTA FRIED ONION RINGS

Prep Time: 10 minutes • Start to Finish: 30 minutes • Makes 4 servings

2 large white onions

1 cup club soda

½ cup beer

1 egg white, whisked until frothy

2¼ to 2½ cups all-purpose flour, divided

1 tablespoon cornstarch

1 packet (1.25 ounces) ORTEGA® Reduced Sodium Chili Seasoning Mix, divided

Vegetable oil for frying

1 cup prepared queso sauce or cheese sauce

CUT peeled onions into ½-inch slices; separate into rings. Set aside.

COMBINE club soda, beer and egg white in large bowl; mix well. Add 1½ cups flour, cornstarch and 2 tablespoons seasoning mix; stir until well combined. Let stand 15 minutes.

HEAT oil in large saucepan to 350°F. Line baking pan with paper towels.

PLACE remaining ¾ cup flour in shallow pan or plate. Dip each onion ring into flour; coat evenly and shake off excess flour. (Use additional ¼ cup flour, if necessary.) Dip floured onion rings in small batches into prepared batter, allowing excess batter to drain. Carefully lower into hot oil using long-handled fork.

FRY 3 minutes or until golden brown. Remove with slotted spoon and drain on paper towels.

SPRINKLE with remaining seasoning mix. Serve immediately with queso sauce for dipping.

TURKEY MEATBALLS WITH YOGURT-CUCUMBER SAUCE

Makes 40 meatballs

- 2 tablespoons olive oil, divided
- 1 cup finely chopped onion
- 2 cloves garlic, minced
- 1¼ pounds ground turkey or ground lamb
- ½ cup plain dry bread crumbs
- ¼ cup whipping cream
- 1 egg, lightly beaten
- 3 tablespoons plus 2 teaspoons chopped fresh mint, divided
- 1¼ teaspoons salt, divided
- ⅛ teaspoon ground red pepper
- 1 container (6 ounces) plain Greek yogurt
- ½ cup peeled seeded and finely chopped cucumber
- 2 teaspoons grated lemon peel
- 2 teaspoons lemon juice
- Crumbled feta cheese and cucumber wedges (optional)

1. Line two baking sheets with parchment paper. Heat 1 tablespoon oil in medium skillet over medium-high heat. Add onion; cook and stir 3 minutes or until softened. Add garlic; cook and stir 30 seconds. Let cool slightly.

2. Combine turkey, onion mixture, bread crumbs, cream, egg, 3 tablespoons mint, 1 teaspoon salt and red pepper in large bowl; mix well. Shape into 40 meatballs. Place meatballs on prepared baking sheets. Cover with plastic wrap; refrigerate 1 hour.

3. Meanwhile for sauce, combine yogurt, chopped cucumber, remaining 2 teaspoons mint, lemon peel, lemon juice and remaining ¼ teaspoon salt in small bowl.

4. Preheat oven to 400°F. Brush meatballs with remaining 1 tablespoon oil. Bake 15 to 20 minutes or until cooked through, turning once during baking. Serve with sauce, feta and cucumber wedges, if desired.

SWEET AND SAVORY ONION DIP

Makes 3 cups dip

1 tablespoon olive oil

3 onions, diced

2 cups plain Greek yogurt

¼ cup grated Parmesan cheese

2 tablespoons fresh lemon juice

½ teaspoon salt

⅛ teaspoon ground red pepper

Vegetable sticks, crackers and/or chips

1. Heat oil in large nonstick skillet over medium-high heat. Add onions; cook and stir 6 to 8 minutes or until golden brown. Reduce heat to low; cook 15 minutes or until onions are deep golden brown; stirring occasionally.

2. Meanwhile, stir yogurt, cheese, lemon juice, salt and red pepper in large bowl until smooth and well blended. Stir in onions. Cover and refrigerate at least 2 hours before serving.

3. Serve with vegetable sticks, crackers and/or chips for dipping.

EGG SALAD SANDWICHES

Makes 4 servings

6 eggs

2 tablespoons mayonnaise

1½ tablespoons sweet pickle relish

½ cup finely chopped celery

⅛ to ¼ teaspoon salt

Black pepper (optional)

8 slices whole grain bread

1. Place eggs in medium saucepan; add cold water to cover. Bring to a boil over high heat. Immediately reduce heat to low; simmer 10 minutes. Drain and peel eggs under cold water.

2. Cut eggs in half. Place egg yolks in medium bowl. Add mayonnaise and pickle relish; mash with fork until yolk mixture is well blended and creamy. Chop egg whites; add to yolk mixture with celery and salt. Stir until well blended. Season to taste with pepper, if desired.

3. Spread ½ cup egg salad on each of four bread slices; top with remaining bread slices. Slice sandwiches into halves or quarters.

CORN FRITTERS WITH FRESH TOMATO SAUCE

Makes 6 to 8 servings

Tomato Sauce (recipe follows) *or* 1⅓ cups chunky salsa

½ cup all-purpose flour

1 teaspoon sugar

½ teaspoon baking powder

½ teaspoon salt

⅛ teaspoon dried thyme, crushed

Pinch ground red pepper (optional)

1 egg

¼ cup half-and-half or milk

1 cup cooked fresh or frozen corn

Vegetable oil for deep frying

1. Prepare tomato sauce. Set aside.

2. Mix flour, sugar, baking powder, salt, thyme and red pepper, if desired, in large bowl. Whisk egg and half-and-half in small bowl. Stir into flour mixture just until well blended. Stir in corn.

3. Pour ¼ inch of oil in large deep skillet. Heat over medium heat until drop of batter sizzles and turns golden in less than a minute. Drop batter by rounded tablespoons into hot oil. Fry on first side 3 minutes or until golden. Turn and fry 1 minute or until golden. Remove fritters with slotted spoon. Drain on paper towels. Serve hot with tomato sauce.

TOMATO SAUCE

1⅓ cups sauce

1 tablespoon vegetable oil

1 small red onion, very thinly sliced (1 cup)

1 cup grape tomatoes, halved

2 teaspoons balsamic vinegar

1 tablespoon capers

¼ teaspoon sugar

¼ teaspoon salt

⅛ teaspoon black pepper

1. Heat oil in large skillet over medium-high heat. Add onion; cook and stir 3 to 5 minutes or until tender. Add tomatoes. Cook 2 to 3 minutes or until very soft. Remove from heat.

2. Stir in vinegar, capers, sugar, salt and pepper. Serve warm or at room temperature.

DOWN-HOME FRIED OKRA

Makes 4 to 6 servings

¼ cup (½ stick) butter

1 clove garlic, minced

½ cup plain dry bread crumbs

1 package (16 ounces) frozen cut okra, thawed

Salt and black pepper

1. Heat butter in large nonstick skillet until melted and sizzling. Add garlic; cook and stir over medium heat 30 seconds or until fragrant. Add bread crumbs; cook and stir 1 minute or until crumbs are coated with butter.

2. Add okra; cook and stir over medium heat 10 minutes or until okra is tender. Season to taste with salt and pepper.

CLASSIC DEVILED EGGS

Prep Time: 30 minutes • Makes 12 halves

- 6 hard-cooked eggs, halved
- ¼ cup HELLMANN'S® or BEST FOODS® Real Mayonnaise
- 1 teaspoon HELLMANN'S® or BEST FOODS® Dijonnaise™ Creamy Dijon Mustard
- ½ teaspoon white vinegar
- ¼ teaspoon salt

1. Remove egg yolks, reserving egg whites.

2. Mash egg yolks in small bowl. Stir in remaining ingredients. Spoon or pipe into egg whites. Chill, if desired. Garnish, if desired, with parsley and sprinkle with paprika.

VARIATION: For a different taste...add 1 tablespoon pickle relish or finely chopped sweet pickles; OR 2 tablespoons cooked crumbled bacon; OR 1 tablespoon chopped green onion, ¾ teaspoon chili powder and hot pepper sauce to taste.

SUBSTITUTION: Also terrific with HELLMANN'S® or BEST FOODS® Canola Cholesterol Free Mayonnaise.

TIP: Make a double recipe because this party classic disappears fast!

TIP: To easily fill eggs, spoon filling into small resealable plastic bag and cut a small hole in one corner. Pipe into egg whites.

DRINKS

FUZZY NAVEL

Makes 1 serving

- 4 ounces orange juice
- 1½ ounces peach schnapps
- 1 ounce vodka (optional)
- Orange slice

Fill cocktail shaker half full with ice; add orange juice, schnapps and vodka, if desired. Shake until blended; strain into ice-filled glass. Garnish with orange slice.

MINT JULEP

Makes 1 serving

- 4 to 6 mint leaves
- 1 teaspoon sugar
- 3 ounces bourbon
- Sprig fresh mint

Muddle mint leaves and sugar in glass. Fill glass with ice; pour in bourbon. Garnish with mint sprig.

WHITE SANGRIA

Makes 8 to 10 servings

- 2 oranges, cut into ¼-inch slices
- 2 lemons, cut into ¼-inch slices
- ½ cup sugar
- 2 bottles (750 ml each) dry, fruity white wine (such as Pinot Grigio), chilled
- ½ cup peach schnapps
- 3 ripe peaches, pit removed and cut into wedges
- 2 cups ice cubes (about 16 cubes)

1. Place orange and lemon slices in large punch bowl. Pour sugar over orange and lemon slices. Mash lightly until sugar dissolves and fruit begins to break down.

2. Stir in wine, peach schnapps and peaches. Refrigerate at least 2 hours or up to 10. Add ice cubes just before serving.

WHISKEY SOUR

Makes 1 serving

- 2 ounces whiskey
- Juice of ½ lemon
- 1 teaspoon powdered sugar *or* 1 tablespoon simple syrup
- Lemon or orange slice and maraschino cherry

Fill cocktail shaker half full with ice; add whiskey, lemon juice and powdered sugar. Shake until blended; strain into ice-filled old fashioned glass. Garnish with lemon slice and maraschino cherry.

VARIATION: Fill cocktail shaker half full with ice; add 4 ounces sweet and sour mix and 1½ ounces whiskey. Shake until blended; strain into ice-filled old fashioned glass. Garnish with lemon slice and maraschino cherry.

SWEET TEA

━━ Makes 1 gallon ━━

1 gallon (16 cups) water

2 cups sugar

8 black tea bags

1. Bring water to a boil in large saucepan or stockpot. Place sugar in large heatproof bowl. Pour about half of hot water into sugar; stir until dissolved. Add tea bags to remaining water in pot. Let steep 15 minutes. Discard tea bags.

2. Pour sugar mixture into tea. Cool to room temperature. Transfer to large pitcher or jars; refrigerate until cold.

PLANTER'S PUNCH

━━ Makes 1 serving ━━

3 ounces orange juice

2 ounces dark rum

Juice of ½ lime

2 teaspoons powdered sugar

¼ teaspoon grenadine

Orange slices and fresh strawberry

Fill cocktail shaker half full with ice; add orange juice, rum, lime juice, sugar and grenadine. Shake until blended; strain into chilled ice-filled glass. Garnish with orange slices and strawberry.

POMEGRANATE CHAI ICED TEA

=== Makes 4 servings ===

- 3 cups water, divided
- 2 spiced chai tea bags
- 1 cup blueberry pomegranate juice
- 3 to 4 tablespoons sugar
- 2 tablespoons lemon juice

1. Bring 1 cup water to a boil in small saucepan over high heat. Remove from heat. Add tea bags. Steep 3 minutes. Discard tea bags.

2. Place pomegranate juice, sugar and lemon juice in pitcher; mix well. Add brewed tea; stir. Serve immediately over ice, or cover and chill.

HURRICANE

=== Makes 1 serving ===

- 2 ounces light rum
- 2 ounces dark rum
- 1 ounce passion fruit juice
- 1 ounce orange juice
- 1 ounce lime juice
- ½ ounce grenadine (optional)

  Pineapple wedges and maraschino cherry

Fill cocktail shaker half full with ice; add rum, juices and grenadine, if desired. Shake until blended; strain into ice-filled glass. Garnish with pineapple wedges and cherry.

BREAKFAST AND BRUNCH

BACON-CHEESE GRITS

2 cups milk

½ cup quick-cooking grits

1½ cups (6 ounces) shredded sharp Cheddar cheese *or* 6 slices American cheese, torn into bite-size pieces

2 tablespoons butter

1 teaspoon Worcestershire sauce

½ teaspoon salt

⅛ teaspoon ground red pepper (optional)

4 thick-cut slices bacon, crisp-cooked and chopped

1. Bring milk to a boil in large saucepan over medium-high heat. Slowly stir in grits; return to a boil. Reduce heat to low; cover and simmer 5 minutes, stirring frequently.

2. Remove from heat; stir in cheese, butter, Worcestershire sauce, salt and red pepper, if desired. Cover and let stand 2 minutes or until cheese is melted. Top with bacon.

VARIATION: For a thinner consistency, add an additional ½ cup milk.

CHICKEN AND WAFFLES WITH SRIRACHA MAPLE SYRUP

Makes 4 to 6 servings

CHICKEN

- ½ cup milk
- 1 egg
- 1¼ pounds chicken tenderloin, about 8 pieces
- 1½ cups panko bread crumbs
- 1 teaspoon paprika
- 1 teaspoon garlic powder
- 1 teaspoon salt
- ½ teaspoon black pepper
- ¼ cup vegetable oil

WAFFLES

- 2 cups biscuit baking mix
- 1⅓ cups milk
- 1 egg

SYRUP

- ½ cup pure maple syrup
- 2 teaspoons sriracha hot sauce
- 4 tablespoons melted butter

1. Whisk ½ cup milk and 1 egg in medium bowl. Add chicken; toss until well coated.

2. Combine panko, paprika, garlic powder, salt and pepper in shallow pie pan. Coat chicken, one at a time, in panko mixture, pressing lightly to adhere. Place on plate.

3. Heat oil in large nonstick skillet over medium-high heat. Reduce heat to medium; cook chicken 6 minutes on each side or until golden brown and no longer pink in center. Remove to plate; keep warm.

4. Preheat waffle maker to medium; spray grid with nonstick cooking spray. Combine baking mix, 1⅓ cups milk and egg in medium bowl. Pour ¾ cup batter in waffle maker; cook 3 to 4 minutes or until golden brown. Remove to serving plate. Repeat with remaining batter.

5. Meanwhile, combine syrup and sriracha in small bowl. Top waffles with chicken tenders. Drizzle with syrup and melted butter.

EGGS BENEDICT WITH SMOKED SALMON

4 English muffins, split and toasted

4 ounces sliced smoked salmon

8 tomato slices

1 teaspoon white vinegar

8 eggs

Hollandaise Sauce (recipe follows)

4 teaspoons chopped fresh dill

1. Preheat oven to 200°F. Place 2 muffin halves, split side up, on each of 4 serving plates. Top with smoked salmon and tomato slices. Place plates in oven; turn off oven.

2. Fill large skillet with 2 inches of water and vinegar; bring to a simmer over medium heat. Break 4 eggs into 4 ramekins or small bowls. Holding ramekins close to surface of water, slip eggs into water.

3. Cook eggs until whites are completely set and yolks begin to thicken but are not hard, about 3 minutes. With slotted spoon, remove eggs; drain over paper towel. Repeat with remaining eggs. Place 1 egg on each prepared muffin half.

4. Prepare Hollandaise Sauce; spoon generous tablespoonful of sauce over each egg. Sprinkle with fresh dill; serve immediately.

HOLLANDAISE SAUCE

Makes about 1 cup

3 egg yolks

¼ cup water

2 tablespoons lemon juice

½ cup (1 stick) cold butter, cut into 8 pieces

¼ teaspoon salt

1. Gently whisk egg yolks, water and lemon juice in small saucepan over low heat 4 minutes or until mixture begins to bubble around edges.

2. Whisk in butter, one piece at a time, until butter is melted and sauce has thickened. Whisk in salt. Do not allow sauce to boil. Serve immediately.

BISCUITS AND GRAVY

Makes 8 servings

- 3 tablespoons canola or vegetable oil, divided
- 8 ounces bulk breakfast sausage
- 2¼ cups plus 3 tablespoons biscuit baking mix, divided
- 2⅔ cups whole milk, divided
- ¼ teaspoon salt
- ¼ teaspoon black pepper

1. Preheat oven to 450°F. Heat 1 tablespoon oil in large nonstick skillet over medium heat. Add sausage; cook and stir until browned, breaking up larger pieces. Remove to plate with slotted spoon.

2. Add remaining 2 tablespoons oil to skillet. Add 3 tablespoons biscuit mix; whisk until smooth. Gradually add 2 cups milk; cook and stir 3 to 4 minutes or until mixture comes to a boil. Cook 1 minute or until thickened, stirring constantly. Add sausage and any accumulated juices; cook and stir 2 minutes. Season with salt and pepper.

3. Combine remaining 2¼ cups biscuit mix and ⅔ cup milk in medium bowl; stir until blended. Spoon batter into 8 mounds onto ungreased nonstick baking sheet.

4. Bake 8 to 10 minutes or until golden. Serve warm with gravy.

CHORIZO HASH

2 unpeeled russet potatoes, cut into ½-inch pieces

1 tablespoon salt, divided

8 ounces chorizo sausage

1 yellow onion, chopped

½ red bell pepper, chopped (about ½ cup)

Avocado slices (optional)

1. Fill medium saucepan half full with water. Add potatoes and 2 teaspoons salt; bring to a boil over high heat. Reduce heat to medium-low; cook about 8 minutes. (Potatoes will be firm.) Drain.

2. Meanwhile, remove and discard casing from chorizo. Crumble chorizo into large (12-inch) cast iron skillet; cook and stir over medium-high heat about 5 minutes or until lightly browned. Add onion and bell pepper; cook and stir about 4 minutes or until vegetables are softened.

3. Stir in potatoes and remaining 1 teaspoon salt; cook 10 to 15 minutes or until vegetables are tender and potatoes are lightly browned, stirring occasionally. Garnish with avocado.

SERVING SUGGESTION: Serve with fried, poached or scrambled eggs.

PINEAPPLE UPSIDE DOUGHNUTS

Makes 14 to 16 doughnuts

2¾ cups all-purpose flour
¼ cup cornstarch
1 teaspoon salt
1 teaspoon baking powder
½ teaspoon baking soda
1 cup granulated sugar
2 eggs
¼ cup (½ stick) butter, melted
1 can (8 ounces) crushed pineapple, divided
1½ teaspoons vanilla

½ cup buttermilk
Vegetable oil for frying

TOPPING

½ cup packed brown sugar
2 tablespoons butter
2 tablespoons milk or cream
¼ teaspoon salt
1 cup powdered sugar, sifted
10 to 12 maraschino cherries, cut into eighths

1. Whisk flour, cornstarch, salt, baking powder and baking soda in large bowl.

2. Beat 1 cup granulated sugar and eggs in large bowl with electric mixer on high speed 3 minutes or until pale and thick. Stir in butter, ¼ cup pineapple and vanilla. Add flour mixture alternately with buttermilk, mixing on low speed after each addition. Press plastic wrap directly onto surface of dough; refrigerate at least 1 hour.

3. Pour about 2 inches of oil into Dutch oven or large heavy saucepan; clip deep-fry or candy thermometer to side of pot. Heat over medium-high heat to 360° to 370°F.

4. Meanwhile, generously flour work surface. Turn out dough onto work surface and dust top with flour. Roll dough about ¼-inch thick; cut out doughnuts with floured doughnut cutter. Gather and reroll scraps. Line large wire rack with paper towels.

5. Working in batches, add doughnuts to hot oil. Cook 1 minute per side or until golden brown. Do not crowd the pan and adjust heat to maintain temperature during frying. Cool on wire racks.

6. For topping, combine brown sugar, butter, milk and salt in small saucepan; cook and stir over medium-low heat until melted. Stir in remaining pineapple. Increase heat to medium-high; cook 5 minutes or until thickened, stirring frequently. Remove from heat; stir in powdered sugar. Spoon topping over doughnuts and top with maraschino cherries.

BEIGNET WAFFLES

Makes 2 servings

1 cup pancake baking mix	Juice of 1 lemon
⅔ cup milk	2 tablespoons butter, melted
1 tablespoon vegetable oil	¼ cup powdered sugar
1 egg white	⅔ cup assorted fresh berries

1. Preheat waffle maker to medium; lightly coat grid with nonstick cooking spray.

2. Whisk pancake mix, milk, oil and egg white in large bowl. Pour ¾ cup mixture onto waffle maker; close lid and cook 4 minutes or until puffed and golden brown. Remove to plate; repeat with remaining batter. Cut each waffle into quarters.

3. Squeeze lemon juice over waffles. Drizzle with melted butter; sift powdered sugar over waffles and top with berries.

CORNMEAL PANCAKES

Makes 4 servings

2 cups buttermilk

2 eggs

¼ cup sugar

2 tablespoons butter, melted

1½ cups yellow cornmeal

¾ cup all-purpose flour

1½ teaspoons baking powder

1 teaspoon salt

Blueberries, butter and maple syrup

1. Whisk buttermilk, eggs, sugar and melted butter in large bowl until well blended. Combine cornmeal, flour, baking powder and salt in medium bowl; stir into buttermilk mixture. Let stand 5 minutes.

2. Lightly grease griddle or large skillet; heat over medium heat. Pour batter by ⅓ cupfuls onto griddle. Cook 3 minutes or until tops of pancakes are bubbly and appear dry; turn and cook 2 minutes or until bottoms are golden. Serve with blueberries, butter and syrup.

BAKED PUMPKIN FRENCH TOAST

Makes 6 servings

1 tablespoon butter, softened

1 loaf challah or egg bread (12 to 16 ounces), cut into ¾-inch-thick slices

7 eggs

1¼ cups whole milk

⅔ cup canned pumpkin

1 teaspoon vanilla

½ teaspoon pumpkin pie spice

⅛ teaspoon salt

3 tablespoons sugar

2 teaspoons ground cinnamon

Maple syrup

1. Generously grease 13×9-inch baking dish with butter. Arrange bread slices in dish, fitting slices in tightly.

2. Whisk eggs, milk, pumpkin, vanilla, pumpkin pie spice and salt in medium bowl until well blended. Pour over bread in baking dish; turn slices to coat completely with egg mixture. Cover and refrigerate 8 hours or overnight.

3. Preheat oven to 350°F. Combine sugar and cinnamon in small bowl; mix well. Turn bread slices again; sprinkle generously with cinnamon-sugar.

4. Bake about 30 minutes or until bread is puffy and golden brown. Serve immediately with maple syrup.

CLASSIC HASH BROWNS

Makes 2 servings

1 large russet potato, peeled and grated

¼ teaspoon salt

⅛ teaspoon black pepper

2 tablespoons vegetable oil

1. Heat medium (8-inch) cast iron skillet over medium heat 5 minutes. Combine potato, salt and pepper in small bowl; toss to coat.

2. Add oil to skillet; heat 30 seconds. Spread potato mixture evenly in skillet. Cook about 5 minutes without stirring or until bottom is browned. Turn potatoes; cook 6 to 8 minutes or until golden brown and crispy. Serve immediately.

CINNAMINI MONKEY BREAD

Makes about 16 servings

3 cups all-purpose flour

1 package (¼ ounce) rapid-rise active dry yeast

1 teaspoon salt

1 cup warm water (120°F)

2 tablespoons butter, melted

5 tablespoons butter, very soft, divided

½ cup packed brown sugar

2 teaspoons ground cinnamon

¼ teaspoon coarse salt

1 cup powdered sugar

2 ounces cream cheese, softened

3 tablespoons milk

1. Combine flour, yeast and 1 teaspoon salt in large bowl of stand mixer. Stir in water and 2 tablespoons melted butter to form rough dough. Knead with dough hook at low speed 5 to 7 minutes or until dough is smooth and elastic.

2. Shape dough into a ball. Place in greased bowl; turn to grease top. Cover and let rise in warm place about 1 hour or until doubled in size.

3. Grease 12-cup (10-inch) bundt pan with 1 tablespoon soft butter. Combine brown sugar, cinnamon and coarse salt in shallow bowl. Turn out dough onto lightly floured surface. Roll dough into 24×16-inch rectangle; cut lengthwise into four strips.

4. Spread 1 tablespoon softened butter over each dough strip; sprinkle evenly with cinnamon-sugar, pressing gently to adhere. Starting with long side, roll up dough jelly-roll style; pinch seam to seal. Cut crosswise into 1-inch slices; place slices in prepared pan with cut sides of slices against side of pan. Cover and let rise in warm place 30 minutes or until dough is puffy. Preheat oven to 350°F.

5. Bake 20 to 25 minutes or until bread is firm and lightly browned. Loosen edges of bread with knife; immediately invert onto serving plate. Cool slightly.

6. Meanwhile for glaze, whisk powdered sugar, cream cheese and milk in medium bowl until smooth. Drizzle some of glaze over bread; serve warm with remaining glaze for dipping.

TIP: For regular-size cinnamon rolls, roll out dough but do not cut into four strips. Spread butter over dough and sprinkle with cinnamon-sugar. Roll up tightly, starting from long side. Cut dough into 12 pieces; place cut side down in 13×9-inch baking pan. Cover and let rise at room temperature 30 minutes or in refrigerator overnight. Bake 15 to 20 minutes.

BREAKFAST BISCUIT BAKE

Makes 8 servings

8 ounces bacon, chopped

1 small onion, finely chopped

1 clove garlic, minced

¼ teaspoon red pepper flakes

5 eggs

¼ cup milk

½ cup (2 ounces) shredded white Cheddar cheese, divided

¼ teaspoon salt

⅛ teaspoon ground black pepper

1 package (16 ounces) refrigerated jumbo buttermilk biscuits (8 biscuits)

1. Preheat oven to 425°F. Cook bacon in large (10-inch) cast iron skillet until crisp. Transfer bacon to paper towel-lined plate with slotted spoon. Drain off and reserve drippings, leaving 1 tablespoon in skillet.

2. Add onion, garlic and red pepper flakes to skillet; cook and stir over medium heat about 8 minutes or until onion is very soft. Set aside to cool slightly.

3. Whisk eggs, milk, ¼ cup cheese, salt and black pepper in medium bowl until well blended. Stir in onion mixture.

4. Wipe out any onion mixture remaining in skillet; grease with additional drippings, if necessary. Separate biscuits and arrange in single layer in bottom of skillet. (Bottom of skillet should be completely covered.) Pour egg mixture over biscuits; sprinkle with remaining ¼ cup cheese and cooked bacon.

5. Bake about 25 minutes or until puffed and golden brown. Serve warm.

SOUPS AND STEWS

CURRIED GINGER PUMPKIN SOUP

Makes 8 servings

1 tablespoon vegetable oil

1 Vidalia onion, coarsely chopped

1 large Golden Delicious apple, peeled and coarsely chopped

3 slices (¼-inch) peeled fresh ginger

1½ teaspoons curry powder

2½ to 3 cups vegetable broth, divided

2 cans (15 ounces each) pumpkin puree

1 cup half-and-half

1 teaspoon salt

Black pepper

Roasted salted pumpkin seeds (pepitas)

1. Heat oil in large saucepan over medium heat. Add onion, apple, ginger and curry powder; cook and stir 10 minutes. Add ½ cup broth; cover and simmer 10 minutes or until apple is tender.

2. Pour onion mixture into blender; blend until smooth. Return to saucepan. (Or use hand-held immersion blender.)

3. Add pumpkin, 2 cups broth, half-and-half, salt and pepper; cook until heated through, stirring occasionally. If soup is too thick, add additional broth, a few tablespoons at a time, until soup reaches desired consistency. Sprinkle with pumpkin seeds, if desired.

DEEP BAYOU CHOWDER

Makes 6 servings

1 tablespoon olive oil

1½ cups chopped onions

1 large green bell pepper, chopped

1 large carrot, chopped

8 ounces red potatoes, diced

1 cup corn

1 cup water

½ teaspoon dried thyme

2 cups milk

2 tablespoons chopped parsley

1½ teaspoons seafood seasoning

¾ teaspoon salt

1. Heat oil in Dutch oven over medium-high heat. Add onions, bell pepper and carrot; cook and stir 4 minutes or until onions are translucent.

2. Add potatoes, corn, water and thyme; bring to a boil over high heat. Reduce heat; cover and simmer 15 minutes or until potatoes are tender. Stir in milk, parsley, seasoning and salt. Cook 5 minutes or until heated through (do not boil).

NEW ORLEANS FISH SOUP

Makes 4 servings

1 **pound skinless firm fish fillets, such as grouper, cod or haddock**

1 **can (about 15 ounces) cannellini beans, rinsed and drained**

1 **can (about 14 ounces) chicken broth**

1 **yellow squash, halved lengthwise and sliced**

1 **tablespoon Cajun seasoning**

2 **cans (about 14 ounces each) stewed tomatoes**

½ **cup sliced green onions**

1 **teaspoon grated orange peel**

Salt and black pepper

1. Cut fish into 1-inch pieces. Combine beans, broth, squash and Cajun seasoning in large saucepan. Bring to a boil over high heat. Reduce heat to medium-low.

2. Stir in tomatoes and fish; cover and simmer 3 to 5 minutes or until fish begins to flake when tested with fork. Stir in green onions and orange peel; season with salt and pepper.

SEAFOOD GUMBO

Makes 4 to 6 servings

½ teaspoon garlic powder

½ teaspoon black pepper

½ teaspoon onion powder

⅛ teaspoon dried thyme

2 tablespoons olive oil

2 tablespoons all-purpose flour

2½ cups diced onion

1½ cups diced celery

¾ cup diced red bell pepper

1 clove garlic, finely minced

1 teaspoon hot pepper sauce

1 teaspoon red pepper flakes

1 cup crushed tomatoes

3 cups chicken broth

½ cup cola beverage

6 okra, sliced

6 slices hot coppa,* chopped and fried

1 small can smoked oysters, rinsed and drained

1 cup lump crabmeat

1 cup small raw shrimp

2 fresh plum tomatoes, seeded and chopped

Salt and black pepper

2 cups cooked white or brown rice

Coppa is a cured meat much like salami. It is sometimes called capicola or capicollo. Or substitute with salami or another type of cured pork.

1. Combine garlic powder, black pepper, onion powder and thyme in small bowl; set aside.

2. Heat oil in Dutch oven or large stockpot over low heat; stir in flour. Increase heat to medium-low; cook about 5 minutes or until mixture is brown.

3. Increase heat to medium-high. Add onion, celery and bell pepper; cook and stir 5 minutes or until tender. Stir in garlic; cook 1 minute. Stir in spice mixture, hot pepper sauce and red pepper flakes. Add crushed tomatoes, broth and cola; bring to rolling boil. Add okra; reduce heat and simmer, uncovered, 40 minutes.

4. Add coppa, oysters, crabmeat, shrimp and fresh tomatoes to Dutch oven. Cover and cook 30 minutes over low heat. Season with salt and black pepper. Serve over rice.

BEEF STEW WITH BACON, ONION AND SWEET POTATOES

Makes 4 servings

1 pound beef stew meat, cut into 1-inch chunks

1 can (about 14 ounces) beef broth

2 medium sweet potatoes, peeled and cut into 2-inch pieces*

1 large onion, cut into 1½-inch pieces

2 slices thick-cut bacon, diced

1 teaspoon dried thyme

1 teaspoon salt

¼ teaspoon black pepper

2 tablespoons water

2 tablespoons cornstarch

*Or substitute 12 ounces carrots.

SLOW COOKER DIRECTIONS

1. Coat inside of slow cooker with nonstick cooking spray. Combine beef, broth, sweet potatoes, onion, bacon, thyme, salt and pepper in slow cooker. Cover; cook on LOW 7 to 8 hours or on HIGH 4 to 5 hours.

2. Transfer beef and vegetables to serving bowl with slotted spoon; keep warm.

3. Stir water into cornstarch in small bowl. Stir into cooking liquid. Cover; cook on HIGH 15 minutes or until thickened. To serve, spoon sauce over beef and vegetables.

BAYOU JAMBALAYA

Makes 8 servings

- 2 stalks celery, diced
- 1 onion, diced
- 28 ounces smoked sausage, cut into ¼-inch slices
- 3 cloves garlic, chopped
- 1 red bell pepper, diced
- 1 tablespoon chopped fresh parsley
- 1 teaspoon dried oregano
- 1 teaspoon dried thyme
- ½ teaspoon paprika
- ½ cup cola beverage
- ½ cup dry white wine
- 1 pound uncooked medium shrimp, peeled and deveined
- 3 cups water
- 1 can (14 ounces) diced tomatoes, undrained
- 1½ cups uncooked long-grain rice
- 1 bay leaf

1. Combine celery, onion and sausage in large skillet over medium-high heat; cook and stir 5 minutes. Add garlic and bell pepper; cook and stir 3 to 4 minutes. Add parsley, oregano, thyme and paprika; cook and stir 1 minute.

2. Add cola and wine, stirring to scrape up browned bits from bottom of pan. Stir in shrimp, water, tomatoes, rice and bay leaf. Increase heat to high; bring to a boil. Reduce heat; cover and simmer 25 minutes or until rice is tender. Remove and discard bay leaf.

TIP: You can make jambalaya with beef, pork, chicken, duck, shrimp, oysters, crayfish, sausage or any combination.

CHILLED CUCUMBER SOUP

Makes 4 servings

1 large cucumber, peeled and coarsely chopped

¾ cup sour cream

¼ cup packed fresh dill

½ teaspoon salt

⅛ teaspoon white pepper (optional)

1½ cups vegetable broth

1. Place cucumber in food processor; process until finely chopped. Add sour cream, dill, salt and white pepper, if desired; process until fairly smooth.

2. Transfer mixture to large bowl; stir in broth. Cover and chill at least 2 hours or up to 24 hours before serving.

MEAT DISHES

PULLED PORK WITH HONEY-CHIPOTLE BARBECUE SAUCE

Makes 8 servings

1 tablespoon chili powder, divided

1 teaspoon chipotle chili powder, divided

1 teaspoon ground cumin, divided

1 teaspoon garlic powder, divided

1 teaspoon salt

1 bone-in pork shoulder (3½ pounds), trimmed

1 can (15 ounces) tomato sauce

5 tablespoons honey, divided

SLOW COOKER DIRECTIONS

1. Coat inside of slow cooker with nonstick cooking spray. Combine 1 teaspoon chili powder, ½ teaspoon chipotle chili powder, ½ teaspoon cumin, ½ teaspoon garlic powder and salt in small bowl. Rub chili powder mixture all over pork. Place pork in slow cooker.

2. Combine tomato sauce, 4 tablespoons honey, remaining 2 teaspoons chili powder, ½ teaspoon chipotle chili powder, ½ teaspoon cumin and ½ teaspoon garlic powder in large bowl. Pour tomato mixture over pork in slow cooker. Cover; cook on LOW 8 hours.

3. Transfer pork to large bowl; cover loosely with foil. *Turn slow cooker to HIGH.* Partially cover and cook on HIGH 30 minutes or until sauce is thickened. Stir in remaining 1 tablespoon honey. Turn off heat.

4. Shred pork using two forks; discard bone. Stir pork back into slow cooker to coat with sauce.

GRILLED RIBS

Makes 4 servings

- 4 pounds pork loin back ribs
- 2 tablespoons paprika
- 2 teaspoons dried basil
- ½ teaspoon onion powder
- ¼ teaspoon garlic powder
- ¼ teaspoon ground red pepper
- ¼ teaspoon black pepper

- 2 sheets (24×18 inches each) heavy-duty foil, lightly sprayed with nonstick cooking spray
- 8 ice cubes
- 1 cup barbecue sauce
- ½ cup apricot fruit spread

1. Prepare grill for direct cooking. Cut ribs into 4- to 6-rib portions.

2. Combine paprika, basil, onion powder, garlic powder, red pepper and black pepper in small bowl. Rub all over both sides of ribs. Place half of ribs in single layer in center of each foil sheet; top each with 4 ice cubes. Double-fold sides and ends of foil to seal packets, leaving head space for heat circulation.

3. Transfer packets to grid. Grill, covered, over medium heat 45 to 60 minutes or until tender. Carefully open one end of each packet to allow steam to escape.

4. Combine barbecue sauce and fruit spread in small bowl. Transfer ribs to grid. Brush with barbecue sauce mixture. Grill 5 to 10 minutes, brushing with sauce and turning often.

SUNDAY BEEF BRISKET

Makes 8 servings

- 1 large onion, thinly sliced
- 1 beef brisket (2 to 2½ pounds), trimmed
- Salt and black pepper
- ⅔ cup chili sauce, divided
- 1½ tablespoons packed brown sugar
- ¼ teaspoon ground cinnamon
- 2 large sweet potatoes, cut into 1-inch pieces
- 1 cup (5 ounces) pitted prunes
- 2 tablespoons cold water
- 2 tablespoons cornstarch

SLOW COOKER DIRECTIONS

1. Place onion in slow cooker; top with brisket. Sprinkle with salt and pepper; top with ⅓ cup chili sauce. Cover; cook on HIGH 3½ hours.

2. Combine remaining ⅓ cup chili sauce, brown sugar and cinnamon in large bowl. Add potatoes and prunes; toss to coat. Pour mixture over brisket. Cover; cook on HIGH 1½ hours.

3. Remove brisket to large cutting board. Cover loosely with foil; let stand 10 to 15 minutes before slicing. Transfer potato mixture to large bowl with slotted spoon; keep warm.

4. Stir water into cornstarch in small bowl until smooth; whisk into cooking liquid. Cover; cook on HIGH 10 to 15 minutes or until sauce is thickened. Serve brisket with potato mixture and sauce.

SPICY BUTTERMILK OVEN-FRIED CHICKEN

Makes 6 servings

1 whole chicken (3½ pounds), cut up

2 cups buttermilk

1½ cups all-purpose flour

1 teaspoon salt

1 teaspoon ground red pepper

½ teaspoon garlic powder

¼ cup canola oil

1. Place chicken pieces in single layer in 13×9-inch baking dish. Pour buttermilk over chicken. Cover with plastic wrap. Marinate in refrigerator at least 2 hours.

2. Preheat oven to 350°F. Combine flour, salt, red pepper and garlic powder in large shallow bowl. Heat oil in large skillet over medium-high heat until hot.

3. Remove chicken pieces from buttermilk; coat with flour mixture. Place chicken in hot oil; cook about 10 minutes or until brown and crisp on all sides. Place chicken in single layer on sheet pan. Bake 30 to 45 minutes or until chicken is cooked through (165°F).

HAM WITH FRUITED BOURBON SAUCE

Makes 10 to 12 servings

1 bone-in ham (about 6 pounds)

¾ cup packed dark brown sugar

½ cup raisins

½ cup apple juice

1 teaspoon ground cinnamon

¼ teaspoon red pepper flakes

⅓ cup dried cherries

¼ cup bourbon, rum or apple juice

¼ cup cornstarch

SLOW COOKER DIRECTIONS

1. Coat inside of slow cooker with nonstick cooking spray. Place ham in slow cooker. Combine brown sugar, raisins, apple juice, cinnamon and red pepper flakes in small bowl; stir well. Pour over ham. Cover; cook on LOW 9 to 10 hours or on HIGH 4½ to 5 hours. Add cherries during last 30 minutes of cooking.

2. Transfer ham to cutting board. Cover loosely with foil; let stand 15 minutes before slicing.

3. Meanwhile, pour cooking liquid into large measuring cup. Let stand 5 minutes; skim and discard fat. Return cooking liquid to slow cooker.

4. *Turn slow cooker to HIGH.* Stir bourbon into cornstarch in small bowl until smooth. Stir into cooking liquid. Cover; cook 15 minutes or until thickened. Serve sauce over ham.

PEACH-GLAZED DUCK BREAST WITH CREOLE RICE

Makes 4 servings

- 2 tablespoons olive oil
- ½ cup chopped onion
- ½ cup chopped celery
- 3 cloves garlic, minced
- 1 cup long-grain white rice or basmati rice
- 1 can (about 14 ounces) chicken broth
- 1 teaspoon Creole, Cajun or blackened redfish seasoning mix
- 4 boneless duck breasts (6 to 7 ounces each) with skin, thawed if frozen
- 1 teaspoon dried thyme
- ½ teaspoon salt
- ¼ teaspoon black pepper
- ⅓ cup peach preserves
- 1½ tablespoons bourbon or whiskey

1. Heat oil in large skillet over medium heat. Add onion, celery and garlic; cook and stir 5 minutes or until onion is translucent. Add rice; cook and stir 30 seconds. Stir in broth and seasoning mix. Bring to a simmer over high heat. Reduce heat; cover and simmer 18 minutes or until liquid is absorbed.

2. Meanwhile, preheat oven to 350°F. Using a sharp knife, score skin of duck breasts in a crisscross pattern; do not cut through to the meat. Heat large cast iron skillet over medium heat 1 minute. Place duck in skillet skin-side down. Sprinkle with thyme, salt and pepper. Cook 9 to 10 minutes or until skin is crispy and golden brown. Turn and cook 3 minutes. Pour off drippings.

3. Combine preserves and bourbon in small bowl; spoon over duck. Transfer skillet to oven. Bake 12 to 14 minutes or until internal temperature reaches 155°F. Transfer duck to cutting board; tent with foil and let stand 5 minutes. (Internal temperature of duck will rise by about 5°F). Place skillet with drippings over medium heat; simmer 2 to 3 minutes or until thickened.

4. Spoon rice onto four serving plates. Carve duck crosswise into thin slices; arrange over rice. Spoon sauce over duck.

FRIED BUTTERMILK CHICKEN FINGERS

Makes 4 servings

CHICKEN

- 1½ cups biscuit baking mix
- 1 cup buttermilk
- 1 egg, beaten
- 12 chicken tenders (about 1½ pounds)
- ½ cup canola or vegetable oil, divided
- Salt and black pepper

DIPPING SAUCE

- ⅓ cup mayonnaise
- 1 tablespoon packed dark brown sugar
- 1 tablespoon honey
- 1 tablespoon mustard

1. Preheat oven to 200°F or "warm" setting. Place biscuit mix in shallow bowl. Whisk buttermilk and egg in another shallow bowl until well blended.

2. Coat chicken pieces in biscuit mix; place on baking sheet. Dip each chicken piece in buttermilk mixture and roll in biscuit mix again to coat evenly; return to baking sheet.

3. Heat ¼ cup oil in large cast iron skillet over medium-high heat until hot. Place half of chicken pieces in skillet. Reduce heat to medium; sprinkle lightly with salt and pepper. Cook 5 to 6 minutes on each side or until golden. Transfer to clean baking sheet. Sprinkle with salt and pepper again, if desired. Keep warm in oven. Repeat with remaining oil and chicken.

4. For dipping sauce, combine mayonnaise, brown sugar, honey and mustard in small bowl. Serve with chicken.

PORK CHOPS WITH BELL PEPPERS AND SWEET POTATO

=== Makes 4 servings ===

- 4 pork loin chops (about 1 pound), ½ inch thick
- 1 teaspoon lemon pepper
- 1 tablespoon vegetable oil
- ½ cup water
- 1 tablespoon lemon juice
- 1 teaspoon dried fines herbes, crushed
- ½ teaspoon beef bouillon granules
- 1¼ cups red and/or yellow bell pepper strips
- 1 cup sliced sweet potato (1-inch pieces)
- ¾ cup sliced Vidalia or other sweet onion
- Hot cooked rice

1. Trim fat from chops. Rub lemon pepper over both sides of pork. Heat oil in large skillet over medium-high heat. Add pork; cook 5 minutes until browned on both sides.

2. Combine water, lemon juice, fines herbes and bouillon granules in small bowl; pour over pork. Reduce heat to medium-low; cover and simmer 5 minutes.

3. Add bell pepper, sweet potato and onion to skillet; return to a boil. Reduce heat. Cover and simmer 10 to 15 minutes or until pork is slightly pink in center and vegetables are crisp-tender. Transfer pork and vegetables to plate with slotted spoon; keep warm.

4. Bring remaining juices in skillet to a boil over high heat. Reduce heat to medium. Cook and stir until mixture thickens slightly, stirring occasionally. Serve pork, vegetables and sauce over rice.

SOUTHERN-STYLE CHICKEN AND GREENS

Makes 4 to 6 servings

1 teaspoon salt

1 teaspoon paprika

½ teaspoon black pepper

3½ pounds bone-in chicken pieces

4 thick slices smoked bacon (4 ounces), cut crosswise into ¼-inch strips

1 cup uncooked white rice

1 can (14½ ounces) stewed tomatoes, undrained

1¼ cups chicken broth

2 cups packed coarsely chopped fresh collard greens, mustard greens or kale (3 to 4 ounces)

1. Preheat oven to 350°F. Combine salt, paprika and pepper in small bowl; sprinkle over chicken.

2. Cook and stir bacon in Dutch oven over medium heat until crisp. Transfer to paper towel-lined plate with slotted spoon, leaving drippings in Dutch oven.

3. Cook chicken in drippings in Dutch oven in single layer; do not crowd pan. Transfer chicken to plate. Drain all but 1 tablespoon drippings from Dutch oven.

4. Add rice to drippings; cook and stir 1 minute. Add tomatoes with juice, broth, greens and half of bacon; bring to a boil over high heat. Remove from heat; arrange chicken over rice mixture.

5. Cover and bake about 40 minutes or until chicken is cooked through (165°F) and most of liquid is absorbed. Let stand 5 minutes before serving. Sprinkle with remaining bacon.

POT ROAST

Makes 6 to 8 servings

1 tablespoon vegetable oil

1 boneless beef chuck shoulder roast (3 to 4 pounds)

6 medium potatoes, halved

6 carrots, sliced

2 onions, quartered

2 stalks celery, sliced

1 can (about 14 ounces) diced tomatoes

Salt and black pepper

Dried oregano

2 tablespoons all-purpose flour

SLOW COOKER DIRECTIONS

1. Heat oil in large skillet over medium heat. Add roast; brown on all sides. Transfer to slow cooker.

2. Add potatoes, carrots, onions, celery and tomatoes. Season with salt, pepper and oregano. Add ½ inch of water to slow cooker. Cover; cook on LOW 8 to 10 hours. Transfer roast to cutting board. Let stand 15 minutes. Remove vegetables with slotted spoon to large bowl; keep warm.

3. Pour juices from slow cooker into small saucepan. Whisk in flour until smooth. Cook and stir over medium heat until thickened. Slice roast, serve with gravy and vegetables.

PORK TENDERLOIN ROAST WITH FIG SAUCE

Makes 4 servings

1 **tablespoon olive oil**	1 **teaspoon dried rosemary**
1 **pork tenderloin roast (about 1 pound)**	½ **teaspoon black pepper**
2 **cloves minced garlic**	1 **jar (about 8 ounces) fig jam or preserves**
1 **teaspoon salt**	¼ **cup dry red wine**

1. Preheat oven to 375°F. Heat oil in large skillet over medium heat. Brown pork on all sides. Place in shallow roasting pan. Sprinkle with garlic, salt, rosemary and pepper. Roast 15 minutes.

2. Meanwhile, combine fig jam and wine in same skillet; cook and stir over low heat 5 minutes or until jam is melted and mixture is warm.

3. Brush small amount of fig sauce over tenderloin; roast 5 to 10 minutes or until temperature reaches 145°F on instant read thermometer. Transfer roast to cutting board. Tent with foil; let stand 10 minutes.

4. Cut pork into thin slices. Serve with remaining fig sauce.

HONEY WHISKEY CLOVE HAM

Makes 10 to 12 servings

¾ cup honey

1½ tablespoons bourbon whiskey

½ teaspoon ground cloves

1 bone-in spiral sliced ham (about 5 pounds)

1. Preheat oven to 275°F. Combine honey, bourbon and cloves in small bowl until well blended. Place ham, cut-side down, in roasting pan; brush with some of honey mixture. Cover with foil.

2. Bake about 1 hour or until heated through. Remove foil from ham. *Increase oven temperature to 425°F.* Brush with honey mixture. Bake about 10 minutes more or until ham is golden brown. Remove from oven and place on serving platter. Pour juices over ham.

CORNISH HENS WITH ANDOUILLE STUFFING

Makes 4 servings

4 Cornish game hens (about 1¼ pounds each), thawed if frozen

6 tablespoons butter, divided

2 links (8 ounces) fully cooked andouille or chicken andouille sausage, chopped

1 cup chopped onion

½ cup thinly sliced celery

1¼ to 1½ cups water

1 bag (8 ounces) herb stuffing mix

1 teaspoon dried thyme

1 teaspoon paprika or smoked paprika

1 teaspoon garlic salt

¼ teaspoon black pepper

1 cup cranberry chutney or whole-berry cranberry sauce

1. Preheat oven to 375°F. Grease 3-quart baking dish. Pat hens dry with paper towels.

2. Melt 2 tablespoons butter in large saucepan over medium heat. Add sausage, onion and celery; cook 8 to 10 minutes or until vegetables are tender and sausage is browned, stirring occasionally. Add water (use 1½ cups water for a moister stuffing); bring to a boil. Remove from heat; add stuffing mix and toss well to combine.

3. Spoon ½ cup stuffing into each hen cavity. Place hens on rack in shallow roasting pan. Tie legs together, if desired. Place remaining stuffing in prepared baking dish.

4. Melt remaining 4 tablespoons butter in small saucepan over low heat. Add thyme, paprika, garlic salt and pepper; mix well. Spoon half of butter mixture over hens. Roast hens 30 minutes. Bake remaining stuffing with hens 25 minutes. Brush remaining butter mixture over hens. Roast 20 to 25 minutes more or until instant-read thermometer reaches 180°F when tested in the thigh. Serve hens and stuffing with cranberry chutney.

ORANGE-ROASTED TURKEY POT ROAST AND VEGETABLES

Cook Time: 1 hour · Makes 4 to 5 servings

- 1½ pounds JENNIE-O TURKEY STORE® Turkey Breast Roast
- 8 medium-size red new potatoes, cut in quarters
- 1 cup frozen pearl onions or 2 small onions, cut in wedges
- 2 medium carrots cut in quarters lengthwise, then in 2-inch pieces
- Salt and pepper

- 1 medium orange
- 1 cup chicken broth
- ½ teaspoon each minced garlic and crushed dried rosemary
- 1 package (9 ounces) frozen artichoke hearts, thawed and separated
- 1 jar (2 ounces) pimiento-stuffed olives, drained
- Fresh rosemary and grated orange peel (optional)

Heat oven to 350°F. In roasting pan, place turkey roast, pop-up timer on top. Surround turkey with potatoes, onions and carrots. Season with salt and pepper to taste. Grate peel from orange, then squeeze juice and pour broth over meat and vegetables. Sprinkle with garlic and rosemary. Bring mixture to a boil on rangetop; cover roasting pan and place in oven. Bake 30 minutes. Stir artichokes and olives into vegetables. Bake until timer pops, 10 to 20 minutes longer. Remove roast and vegetables to serving platter. Place roasting pan over high heat and boil juices until reduced by half. To serve, spoon juices over sliced turkey and vegetables. Garnish with fresh rosemary and grated orange peel, if desired.

NOTE: If you're doubling the recipe and using a larger roast (3 to 4 pounds), don't add potatoes, onions and carrots until roast has cooked for an hour, or the vegetables will be overcooked. Baste the vegetables with pan drippings after adding them, then continue cooking as directed in recipe.

COUNTRY CAPTAIN CHICKEN

Makes 4 servings

4 boneless skinless chicken
  thighs

2 tablespoons all-purpose
  flour

2 tablespoons vegetable oil,
  divided

1 cup chopped green bell
  pepper

1 onion, chopped

1 stalk celery, chopped

1 clove garlic, minced

¼ cup chicken broth

2 cups canned crushed
  tomatoes or diced fresh
  tomatoes

½ cup golden raisins

1½ teaspoons curry powder

1 teaspoon salt

¼ teaspoon paprika

¼ teaspoon black pepper

Hot cooked rice

SLOW COOKER DIRECTIONS

1. Combine chicken and flour in large resealable food storage bag. Seal bag and shake to coat. Heat 1 tablespoon oil in large skillet over medium-high heat. Add bell pepper, onion, celery and garlic; cook and stir 5 minutes or until vegetables are tender. Transfer to slow cooker.

2. Heat remaining 1 tablespoon oil in same skillet over medium-high heat. Add chicken; cook 5 minutes per side or until browned. Transfer to slow cooker.

3. Pour broth into skillet. Cook and stir over medium-high heat, stirring to scrape up browned bits from bottom of skillet. Pour into slow cooker. Add tomatoes, raisins, curry powder, salt, paprika and black pepper. Cover; cook on LOW 3 hours. Serve chicken and sauce over rice.

CAJUN-STYLE COUNTRY RIBS

Makes 6 to 8 servings

2 cups baby carrots

1 onion, coarsely chopped

1 green bell pepper, cut into 1-inch pieces

1 red bell pepper, cut into 1-inch pieces

2 teaspoons minced garlic

2 tablespoons Cajun or Creole seasoning, divided

3½ to 4 pounds pork country-style spareribs

1 can (about 14 ounces) stewed tomatoes, undrained

2 tablespoons water

1 tablespoon cornstarch

Hot cooked rice

SLOW COOKER DIRECTIONS

1. Combine carrots, onion, bell peppers, garlic and 2 teaspoons seasoning in slow cooker; mix well.

2. Trim excess fat from ribs; cut into individual ribs. Sprinkle with 1 tablespoon Cajun seasoning; place in slow cooker. Pour tomatoes over ribs. Cover; cook on LOW 6 to 8 hours.

3. Remove ribs and vegetables from slow cooker with slotted spoon. Let liquid stand 15 minutes; skim off fat.

4. *Turn slow cooker to HIGH.* Stir water into cornstarch and remaining 1 teaspoon seasoning in small bowl until smooth. Add to slow cooker; stir until blended. Cook, uncovered, 15 minutes or until thickened. Return ribs and vegetables to sauce; carefully stir to coat. Serve with rice.

FISH AND SEAFOOD

SOUTHERN CRAB CAKES WITH RÉMOULADE

Makes 8 servings

10 ounces fresh lump crabmeat

1½ cups fresh white or sourdough bread crumbs, divided

¼ cup chopped green onions

½ cup mayonnaise, divided

1 egg white, lightly beaten

2 tablespoons coarse grain or spicy brown mustard, divided

¾ teaspoon hot pepper sauce, divided

2 tablespoons vegetable oil, divided

Lemon wedges (optional)

1. Preheat oven to 200°F. Pick out and discard any shell or cartilage from crabmeat. Combine crabmeat, ¾ cup bread crumbs and green onions in medium bowl. Add ¼ cup mayonnaise, egg white, 1 tablespoon mustard and ½ teaspoon hot pepper sauce; mix well. Shape mixture by ¼ cupfuls into 8 (½-inch-thick) cakes. Roll crab cakes lightly in remaining ¾ cup bread crumbs.

2. Heat 1 tablespoon oil in large cast iron skillet over medium heat. Add 4 crab cakes; cook 4 to 5 minutes per side or until golden brown. Transfer to serving platter; keep warm in oven. Repeat with remaining 1 tablespoon oil and crab cakes.

3. For rémoulade, combine remaining ¼ cup mayonnaise, 1 tablespoon mustard and ¼ teaspoon hot pepper sauce in small bowl; mix well. Serve with crab cakes and lemon wedges, if desired.

BLACKENED CATFISH WITH TARTAR SAUCE

Makes 4 servings

½ cup mayonnaise

¼ cup sweet pickle relish

4 teaspoons lemon juice, divided

4 catfish fillets (4 ounces each)

1 teaspoon olive oil

¼ teaspoon garlic powder

2 teaspoons blackened or Cajun seasoning blend

Hot cooked rice

1. For tartar sauce, combine mayonnaise, relish and 2 teaspoons lemon juice in small bowl; mix well. Cover and refrigerate until ready to serve.

2. Rinse catfish and pat dry. Combine remaining 2 teaspoons lemon juice, oil and garlic powder in small bowl; brush half of mixture over fish. Sprinkle with seasoning blend; brush with remaining lemon juice mixture.

3. Heat large nonstick skillet over medium-high heat. Add two fillets, seasoned side down; cook 3 minutes per side. Reduce heat to medium and cook 3 minutes more or until fish begins to flake when tested with a fork. Remove fillets from skillet; keep warm. Repeat with remaining fillets. Serve with tartar sauce and rice.

BAKED CATFISH WITH PEACH SALSA

Makes 4 servings

4 catfish fillets (4 ounces each), rinsed and patted dry

½ teaspoon salt

½ teaspoon dried Italian seasoning

¼ cup fresh bread crumbs

2 tablespoons butter, melted

½ cup peach salsa

¼ cup coarsely chopped peeled cucumber

1. Preheat oven to 425°F. Spray shallow baking pan with nonstick cooking spray.

2. Place fish in pan; sprinkle with salt and Italian seasoning. Combine bread crumbs and butter in small bowl. Pat mixture onto fish.

3. Bake 20 minutes or until fish begins to flake when tested with fork.

4. Meanwhile, combine salsa and cucumber in small bowl; serve with fish.

SHRIMP AND GARLIC-PARMESAN GRITS

Makes 4 servings

GRITS

- 4 cups water
- 1 cup uncooked old-fashioned or quick grits
- ¼ cup milk
- ¼ cup (½ stick) butter
- ½ cup grated Parmesan cheese
- ½ teaspoon garlic powder
- ½ teaspoon salt

SHRIMP

- 1 teaspoon dried oregano
- ½ teaspoon smoked paprika
- ½ teaspoon dried basil
- ¼ teaspoon salt
- ¼ to ½ teaspoon black pepper
- ⅛ to ¼ teaspoon ground red pepper (optional)
- 1 tablespoon olive oil
- 8 ounces peeled raw shrimp
- ¾ cup chopped green onions
- Lemon wedges (optional)

1. Bring water to a boil in medium saucepan over high heat. Gradually stir in grits; reduce heat. Cover and simmer 20 minutes or until very thick, stirring occasionally. Remove from heat. Stir in milk and butter until blended. Add cheese, ½ teaspoon salt and garlic powder; stir until well blended. Cover; keep warm.

2. Meanwhile, combine oregano, paprika, basil, ¼ teaspoon salt, black pepper and red pepper, if desired, in small bowl. Heat oil in large nonstick skillet over medium-high heat. Add shrimp; sprinkle with oregano mixture. Cook 4 minutes or until shrimp are pink and opaque, stirring frequently. Remove from heat; stir in green onions. Cover to keep warm.

3. Place grits on serving plates; top with shrimp mixture. Serve with lemon wedges, if desired.

BUTTERY CRACKER AND OYSTER CASSEROLE

Makes 12 servings

3 sleeves saltine crackers

1 container (16 ounces) oysters (about 18 oysters total), drained

1 cup (2 sticks) butter, cut into ½-inch cubes

3 cups whole milk

1. Preheat oven to 350°F.

2. Spray 13×9-inch glass baking dish with nonstick cooking spray. Coarsely crush crackers in packages with hands. (Most crumbs should be in ½-inch pieces.) Break seal of one sleeve; sprinkle crumbs into bottom of prepared pan. Arrange half of oysters on top of crumbs. Scatter about one fourth of butter cubes over oysters; drizzle with 1½ cups milk. Repeat layers. Sprinkle with remaining sleeve of crackers and top with remaining butter.

3. Bake 30 minutes or until light golden brown. Let stand 10 minutes before serving. Serve within 30 minutes for peak flavor and texture.

CORNMEAL-CRUSTED CATFISH

Makes 4 servings

½ cup cornmeal

¼ cup crushed pecans

2 teaspoons dried minced onion

1½ teaspoons garlic powder

1 teaspoon salt

1 teaspoon paprika

½ teaspoon black pepper

3 tablespoons mayonnaise

2 tablespoons apricot preserves or fruit spread

1 pound catfish fillets

1 tablespoon vegetable oil

1. Heat medium nonstick skillet over medium heat. Add cornmeal, pecans, onion, garlic powder, salt, paprika and pepper; cook and stir 3 minutes or until cornmeal begins to brown. Transfer to shallow dish.

2. Combine mayonnaise and preserves in small bowl; brush over both sides of catfish. Dredge in toasted cornmeal mixture, turning to coat.

3. Heat oil in same skillet over medium heat. Add catfish; cook 3 to 4 minutes on each side or until fish begins to flake when tested with fork.

PAN-FRIED OYSTERS

Makes 2 to 4 servings

¼ cup all-purpose flour

½ teaspoon salt

¼ teaspoon black pepper

2 eggs

½ cup plain dry bread crumbs

5 tablespoons chopped fresh parsley, divided

2 containers (8 ounces each) shucked fresh oysters, rinsed, drained and patted dry *or* 1 pound fresh oysters, shucked and patted dry

Canola oil for frying

5 slices bacon, crisp-cooked and chopped

Lemon wedges

1. Combine flour, salt and pepper in shallow bowl. Whisk eggs in another shallow bowl. Combine bread crumbs and 4 tablespoons parsley in third shallow bowl.

2. Working with one oyster at a time, coat with flour mixture, shaking off excess. Dip in eggs, shaking off excess; roll in bread crumb mixture to coat. Place coated oysters on plate.

3. Heat ½ inch of oil in large deep skillet over medium-high heat until very hot but not smoking (about 370°F). Add one third of oysters; cook about 2 minutes per side or until golden brown. Drain on paper towel-lined plate. Repeat with remaining oysters.

4. Toss oysters with bacon and remaining 1 tablespoon parsley in large bowl. Serve immediately with lemon wedges.

SHRIMP CREOLE

Makes 4 to 6 servings

2 tablespoons olive oil

1½ cups chopped green bell peppers

1 medium onion, chopped

⅔ cup chopped celery

2 cloves garlic, minced

1 cup uncooked white rice

1 can (about 14 ounces) diced tomatoes, drained and liquid reserved

2 teaspoons hot pepper sauce, or to taste

1 teaspoon dried oregano

¾ teaspoon salt

½ teaspoon dried thyme

Black pepper

1 pound medium raw shrimp, peeled

1 tablespoon chopped fresh parsley (optional)

1. Preheat oven to 325°F. Heat oil in large skillet over medium-high heat. Add bell peppers, onion, celery and garlic; cook and stir 5 minutes or until vegetables are tender.

2. Reduce heat to medium. Add rice; cook and stir 5 minutes. Add tomatoes, hot pepper sauce, oregano, salt, thyme and black pepper to skillet; stir until well blended. Pour reserved tomato liquid into measuring cup. Add enough water to measure 1¾ cups; add to skillet. Cook and stir 2 minutes. Stir in shrimp. Transfer to 2½-quart baking dish.

3. Cover and bake 55 minutes or until rice is tender and liquid is absorbed. Garnish with parsley.

OYSTER PO' BOYS

Makes 4 sandwiches

½ cup mayonnaise

2 tablespoons plain yogurt

1 clove garlic, minced

¼ teaspoon ground red pepper

¾ cup cornmeal

¼ cup all-purpose flour

½ teaspoon salt

⅛ teaspoon black pepper

¾ cup oil for frying

2 pints shucked oysters, drained

4 French bread rolls,* split

Lettuce leaves

Tomato slices

Or substitute French bread loaf, split and cut into 4-inch lengths, for French bread rolls.

1. Combine mayonnaise, yogurt, garlic and red pepper in small bowl; set aside.

2. Combine cornmeal, flour, salt and pepper in shallow bowl.

3. Heat oil in medium skillet over medium heat. Pat oysters dry with paper towels. Dip oysters in cornmeal mixture to coat. Fry in batches 5 minutes or until golden brown, turning once. Drain on paper towel-lined plate.

4. Spread rolls with mayonnaise mixture; fill with lettuce, tomatoes and oysters.

PAN-FRIED CAJUN BASS

2 tablespoons all-purpose flour

1½ teaspoons Cajun or Caribbean jerk seasoning

1 egg white

2 teaspoons water

⅓ cup seasoned dry bread crumbs

2 tablespoons cornmeal

4 skinless striped bass, halibut or cod fillets (4 to 6 ounces each), thawed if frozen

1 teaspoon butter

1 teaspoon olive oil

Chopped fresh parsley

4 lemon wedges

1. Combine flour and seasoning in medium resealable food storage bag. Beat egg white and water in shallow bowl. Combine bread crumbs and cornmeal in another shallow bowl.

2. Working with one at a time, add fillet to bag; shake to coat evenly. Dip in egg white mixture, letting excess drip back into bowl. Roll in bread crumb mixture, pressing lightly to adhere. Repeat with remaining fillets.

3. Melt butter and oil in large nonstick skillet over medium heat. Add fillets; cook 4 to 5 minutes per side or until golden brown and fish is opaque in center and flakes easily when tested with fork. Sprinkle with parsley and serve with lemon wedges.

SALADS

GRILLED STONE FRUIT SALAD

Makes 4 servings

2 tablespoons fresh orange juice

1 tablespoon lemon juice

2 teaspoons canola oil

1 teaspoon honey

½ teaspoon Dijon mustard

1 tablespoon finely chopped fresh mint

1 medium peach, halved and pitted

1 medium nectarine, halved and pitted

1 medium plum, halved and pitted

4 cups mixed baby greens

½ cup crumbled goat cheese

1. Prepare grill for direct cooking over medium-high heat. Spray grid with nonstick cooking spray.

2. For dressing, whisk orange juice, lemon juice, oil, honey and mustard in small bowl until smooth and well blended. Stir in mint.

3. Brush cut sides of fruit with some of dressing; set remaining dressing aside. Grill fruit, cut sides down, covered, 2 to 3 minutes. Turn and grill 2 to 3 minutes or until fruit begins to soften. Transfer to plate; cool slightly. Cut into wedges when cool enough to handle.

4. Arrange greens on four serving plates. Top evenly with fruit and goat cheese. Drizzle with remaining dressing. Serve immediately.

GRILLED ROMAINE HEARTS

Makes 6 servings

VINAIGRETTE

- 1½ cups cola beverage
- 3 tablespoons white vinegar
- 3 tablespoons canola oil
- 2 tablespoons sugar
- ½ teaspoon salt
- ¼ teaspoon onion powder
- ¼ teaspoon garlic powder
- 1½ tablespoons ketchup
- 1½ teaspoons balsamic vinegar
- Dash black pepper
- 1 tablespoon honey mustard

ROMAINE HEARTS

- 6 romaine hearts
- ¼ to ½ cup olive oil
- Salt and black pepper

1. For vinaigrette, whisk cola, white vinegar, canola oil, sugar, ½ teaspoon salt, onion powder, garlic powder, ketchup, balsamic vinegar, mustard and dash pepper in medium bowl.

2. Prepare grill for direct cooking over medium-high heat. Cut romaine hearts in half lengthwise; drizzle with olive oil and sprinkle generously with salt and pepper. Grill about 2 minutes per side or until wilted and lightly charred.

3. Drizzle vinaigrette over romaine. Store remaining vinaigrette in the refrigerator.

TOMATO, AVOCADO AND CUCUMBER SALAD

Makes 4 servings

1½ tablespoons extra virgin olive oil

1 tablespoon balsamic vinegar

1 clove garlic, minced

¼ teaspoon salt

¼ teaspoon black pepper

2 cups diced seeded plum tomatoes

1 small ripe avocado, diced into ½-inch cubes

½ cup chopped cucumber

⅓ cup crumbled feta cheese

4 large red leaf lettuce leaves (optional)

Chopped fresh basil

1. Whisk oil, vinegar, garlic, salt and pepper in medium bowl. Add tomatoes and avocado; toss to coat evenly. Gently stir in cucumber and feta cheese.

2. Arrange lettuce leaves on serving plates, if desired; top with salad and basil.

CRAB COBB SALAD

Makes 8 servings

- 12 cups torn romaine lettuce
- 2 cans (6 ounces each) crabmeat, drained
- 2 cups diced ripe tomatoes or halved cherry tomatoes
- ¼ cup crumbled blue or Gorgonzola cheese
- ¼ cup chopped cooked bacon or imitation bacon bits
- ¾ cup Italian or blue cheese salad dressing
- Black pepper

1. Arrange lettuce on large serving platter or individual serving plates. Arrange crabmeat, tomatoes, blue cheese and bacon bits over lettuce.

2. Just before serving, drizzle dressing evenly over salad. Season with pepper to taste.

NINE-LAYER SALAD

Makes 8 servings

6 cups baby spinach, packed

1½ cups grape tomatoes

2 cups cooked pattypan squash, halved crosswise, or sliced yellow squash

1 cup peas, blanched

4 ounces baby corn, halved lengthwise

2 cups baby carrots, blanched and halved lengthwise

1 cup peppercorn-ranch salad dressing

1 cup (4 ounces) shredded Cheddar cheese

4 slices bacon, crisp-cooked and crumbled

1. Layer spinach, tomatoes, squash, peas, corn and carrots in large glass bowl or trifle dish. Pour dressing over salad; spread evenly. Top with cheese. Cover and refrigerate 4 hours.

2. Sprinkle with bacon before serving.

WILTED SPINACH SALAD WITH WHITE BEANS AND OLIVES

Makes 4 servings

- 2 **thick slices bacon, diced**
- ½ **cup chopped onion**
- 1 **can (about 15 ounces) navy beans, rinsed and drained**
- ½ **cup halved pitted kalamata or black olives**

- 1 **package (9 ounces) baby spinach**
- 1 **cup cherry or grape tomatoes, halved**
- 1½ **tablespoons balsamic vinegar**
- **Black pepper (optional)**

1. Cook bacon in Dutch oven or large saucepan over medium heat 2 minutes. Add onion; cook 5 to 6 minutes or until bacon is crisp and onion is tender, stirring occasionally. Stir in beans and olives; heat through.

2. Add spinach, tomatoes and vinegar; cover and cook 1 minute or until spinach is slightly wilted. Turn off heat; toss lightly. Transfer to serving plates. Season with pepper, if desired.

APPLE-WALNUT SALAD WITH BLUE CHEESE-HONEY VINAIGRETTE

Makes 4 servings

- ¼ cup chopped walnuts
- 1 tablespoon white wine vinegar
- 2 teaspoons olive oil
- 2 teaspoons honey
- ¼ teaspoon salt
- ⅛ teaspoon black pepper

- 2 tablespoons crumbled blue cheese
- 1 large head Bibb lettuce, separated into leaves
- 1 small Red Delicious or other red apple, thinly sliced
- 1 small Granny Smith apple, thinly sliced

1. Place walnuts in small skillet. Cook and stir over medium heat 5 minutes or until fragrant and lightly toasted. Transfer to plate to cool.

2. Whisk vinegar, oil, honey, salt and pepper in small bowl until well blended. Stir in cheese.

3. Divide lettuce and apples evenly among four plates. Drizzle dressing evenly over each salad; top with walnuts.

ZESTY WATERMELON SALAD

½ cup WISH-BONE® Italian Dressing

¼ cup sugar

1 jalapeño pepper, finely chopped (optional)

6 cups cubed watermelon (about 2 lbs.)

1 large seedless cucumber,* halved lengthwise, then sliced (about 3 cups)

¼ cup torn cilantro or mint leaves

Salt and ground black pepper (optional)

If using regular cucumber, remove seeds before slicing.

Stir WISH-BONE® Italian Dressing, sugar and jalapeño pepper in small bowl until sugar is dissolved; set aside.

Combine remaining ingredients in large bowl. Season with salt and black pepper. Just before serving, drain watermelon mixture, then toss with Dressing mixture.

CANTALOUPE CHICKEN SALAD

Makes 2 servings

- 1 package (3 ounces) ramen noodles, crumbled, divided*
- 1 cup diced cooked chicken
- ½ cup seedless red grapes, halved
- ¼ cup chopped green bell pepper
- ¼ cup diced red onion
- 1 large cantaloupe
- 2 tablespoons vegetable oil
- 2 tablespoons sugar
- 1 tablespoon white vinegar

Discard seasoning packet.

1. Combine ½ cup crumbled ramen noodles, chicken, grapes, bell pepper and onion in large bowl; toss until well blended.

2. Cut cantaloupe in half and remove seeds. Scoop out some melon from each half (about ¼ cup each); cut into cubes. Stir into chicken mixture.

3. Whisk oil, sugar and vinegar in small bowl. Pour over salad; toss to coat.

4. Divide salad between cantaloupe halves. Garnish with some of remaining noodles.

SIDE DISHES

GREEN BEAN CASSEROLE

Makes 6 to 8 servings

6 cups water

1 pound fresh green beans, cut into 2-inch pieces

1 tablespoon vegetable oil

8 ounces cremini mushrooms, chopped

3 tablespoons butter

3 tablespoons plus ½ cup all-purpose flour, divided

2 teaspoons salt, divided

¼ teaspoon red pepper flakes

1 cup mushroom or vegetable broth

1½ cups whole milk, divided

2 small onions, sliced into rings

½ cup cornmeal

½ teaspoon black pepper

Vegetable oil for frying

1. Preheat oven to 350°F. Spray 13×9-inch baking dish with nonstick cooking spray.

2. Bring water to a boil in medium saucepan. Add green beans; cook 4 minutes. Drain.

3. Heat oil in large saucepan over medium heat. Add mushrooms; cook and stir 8 minutes or until mushrooms are browned and have released their liquid. Add butter; cook and stir until melted. Stir in 3 tablespoons flour, 1 teaspoon salt and red pepper flakes. Gradually stir in broth and 1 cup milk; cook and stir until thickened. Remove from heat; stir in green beans. Pour into prepared dish. Bake 30 minutes.

4. Meanwhile for onion rings, line baking sheet with paper towels. Separate onion rings and spread in shallow dish. Pour remaining ½ cup milk over onions; toss to coat. Combine remaining ½ cup flour, cornmeal, remaining 1 teaspoon salt and pepper in large resealable food storage bag; mix well.

5. Heat oil in large heavy skillet over medium-high heat until temperature registers 300° to 325°F on deep-fry thermometer.

6. Working in batches, add onion rings to food storage bag; shake to coat. Add onions to oil; fry 2 minutes per side or until golden brown. Transfer to prepared baking sheet with slotted spoon.

7. Remove casserole from oven. Top with onions; bake 5 minutes.

HUSH PUPPIES

Prep Time: 10 minutes • Start to Finish Time: 15 minutes • Makes 12 hush puppies

Vegetable oil for frying
1 cup CREAM OF WHEAT® Hot
   Cereal (Instant, 1-minute,
   2½-minute or 10-minute
   cook time), uncooked

⅓ cup milk
1 egg
¼ cup minced onions
1 tablespoon honey
½ teaspoon salt

1. Preheat oil in deep fryer or heavy saucepan to 360°F. Combine remaining ingredients in medium bowl. Let stand 5 minutes.

2. Using two tablespoons, form batter into 1-inch balls and drop into hot oil. Cook 3 minutes or until brown and crispy. Remove with slotted spoon and drain on paper towels. Serve warm.

TIP: For a sweet treat, sprinkle powdered sugar over the hush puppies before serving.

AMBROSIA

1 can (20 oz.) DOLE®
  Pineapple Chunks, drained

1 can (11 or 15 oz.) DOLE®
  Mandarin Oranges, drained

1 DOLE® Banana, sliced

1½ cups seedless grapes

½ cup miniature marshmallows

1 cup vanilla low-fat yogurt

¼ cup flaked coconut, toasted

• **COMBINE** pineapple chunks, mandarin oranges, banana, grapes and marshmallows in medium bowl.

• **STIR** yogurt into fruit mixture. Sprinkle with coconut.

FARMERS' MARKET POTATO SALAD

Pickled Red Onions (recipe follows)

2 cups cubed assorted potatoes (purple, baby red, Yukon Gold and/or a combination)

1 cup green beans, cut into 1-inch pieces

2 tablespoons plain Greek yogurt

2 tablespoons white wine vinegar

2 tablespoons olive oil

1 tablespoon spicy mustard

1 teaspoon salt

1. Prepare Pickled Red Onions.

2. Bring large saucepan of water to a boil. Add potatoes; cook 5 to 8 minutes or until fork-tender. Add green beans during last 4 minutes of cooking. Drain potatoes and green beans.

3. Whisk yogurt, vinegar, oil, mustard and salt in large bowl until smooth and well blended.

4. Add potatoes, green beans and Pickled Red Onions to dressing; gently toss to coat. Cover and refrigerate at least 1 hour before serving to allow flavors to develop.

PICKLED RED ONIONS

Makes about ½ cup

½ cup thinly sliced red onion

¼ cup white wine vinegar

2 tablespoons water

1 teaspoon sugar

½ teaspoon salt

Combine all ingredients in large glass jar. Seal jar; shake well. Refrigerate at least 1 hour or up to 1 week.

SPINACH-MELON SALAD

6 cups packed fresh spinach

4 cups mixed melon balls (cantaloupe, honeydew and/or watermelon)

1 cup zucchini ribbons*

½ cup sliced red bell pepper

¼ cup thinly sliced red onion

¼ cup red wine vinegar

2 tablespoons honey

2 teaspoons olive oil

2 teaspoons lime juice

1 teaspoon poppy seeds

1 teaspoon dried mint

*To make ribbons, thinly slice zucchini lengthwise with vegetable peeler or spiral cutter.

1. Combine spinach, melon, zucchini, bell pepper and onion in large bowl.

2. Combine vinegar, honey, oil, lime juice, poppy seeds and mint in small jar with tight-fitting lid; shake well. Pour over salad; toss gently to coat.

SWEET POTATO AND PECAN CASSEROLE

Makes 6 to 8 servings

1 can (40 ounces) sweet potatoes, drained and mashed

½ cup apple juice

⅓ cup plus 2 tablespoons butter, melted, divided

½ teaspoon salt

½ teaspoon ground cinnamon

¼ teaspoon black pepper

2 eggs, beaten

⅓ cup chopped pecans

⅓ cup packed brown sugar

2 tablespoons all-purpose flour

SLOW COOKER DIRECTIONS

1. Spray inside of slow cooker with nonstick cooking spray. Combine sweet potatoes, apple juice, ⅓ cup butter, salt, cinnamon and pepper in large bowl. Whisk in eggs. Place mixture into prepared slow cooker.

2. Combine pecans, brown sugar, flour and remaining 2 tablespoons butter in small bowl. Spread over sweet potatoes. Cover; cook on HIGH 3 to 4 hours.

FRIED GREEN TOMATOES

Makes 3 to 4 servings

- 2 medium green tomatoes
- ¼ cup all-purpose flour
- ¼ cup yellow cornmeal
- ½ teaspoon salt
- ½ teaspoon garlic salt
- ½ teaspoon ground red pepper
- ½ teaspoon black pepper
- 1 cup buttermilk
- 1 cup vegetable oil
- Hot pepper sauce (optional)

1. Cut tomatoes into ¼-inch-thick slices. Combine flour, cornmeal, salt, garlic salt, red pepper and black pepper in shallow bowl; mix well. Pour buttermilk into another shallow bowl.

2. Heat oil in large skillet over medium heat to 360°F. Dip tomato slices into buttermilk, coating both sides. Immediately dredge slices in flour mixture; shake off excess.

3. Fry tomato slices 3 to 5 minutes per side. Drain on paper towels. Serve immediately with hot pepper sauce, if desired.

BBQ BAKED BEANS

Makes 12 servings

3 cans (about 15 ounces each) white beans, drained

4 slices bacon, chopped

¾ cup barbecue sauce

½ cup maple syrup

1½ teaspoons ground mustard

SLOW COOKER DIRECTIONS

1. Coat inside of slow cooker with nonstick cooking spray. Add beans, bacon, barbecue sauce, syrup and mustard; stir to blend.

2. Cover; cook on LOW 4 hours, stirring halfway through cooking time.

CREAMY COLESLAW

Makes 8 servings

½ cup mayonnaise

½ cup buttermilk

2 teaspoons sugar

1 teaspoon celery seed

1 teaspoon fresh lime juice

½ teaspoon chili powder

3 cups shredded coleslaw mix

1 cup shredded carrots

¼ cup finely chopped red onion

1. Whisk mayonnaise, buttermilk, sugar, celery seed, lime juice and chili powder in large bowl until smooth and well blended. Add coleslaw mix, carrots and onion; toss to coat evenly.

2. Cover and refrigerate at least 2 hours before serving.

MAC & CHEESIEST

Makes 6 servings

- 8 ounces uncooked elbow macaroni
- ¼ cup (½ stick) butter
- 5 tablespoons all-purpose flour
- 2¾ cups warm milk
- 1 teaspoon salt
- ¼ teaspoon ground nutmeg
- ¼ teaspoon black pepper
- 2 to 3 drops hot pepper sauce (optional)
- 8 ounces (about 2 cups) shredded Cheddar cheese, divided
- 2 ounces (about ½ cup) shredded Gruyère or Swiss cheese
- 2 ounces (about ½ cup) shredded American cheese
- 3 ounces (about ¾ cup) shredded aged Gouda cheese

1. Preheat oven to 350°F. Cook pasta according to package directions until barely al dente. Run under cold running water to stop cooking; drain.

2. Melt butter in large saucepan over medium-low heat until bubbly. Whisk in flour until smooth paste forms; whisk 2 minutes without browning. Gradually whisk in milk; cook 6 to 8 minutes over medium heat, whisking constantly until mixture begins to bubble and thickens slightly. Add salt, nutmeg, black pepper and hot pepper sauce, if desired. Remove from heat. Stir in 1½ cups of Cheddar, Gruyère, American and Gouda cheeses until smooth. Stir in pasta. Transfer to 2-quart baking dish; sprinkle with remaining ½ cup Cheddar cheese.

3. Bake 20 to 30 minutes or until golden brown.

SPICY BLACK-EYED PEAS WITH HAM HOCKS

Makes 6 servings

6 cups water

2 ham hocks (about 1 pound)

2 pounds cooked black-eyed peas

½ cup chopped onion

½ jalapeño pepper, stemmed and sliced in rounds

2 teaspoons salt

Sliced green onions

1. Bring water to a boil over high heat in Dutch oven. Add ham hocks, black-eyed peas, onion, jalapeño pepper and salt; return to a boil. Reduce heat and simmer, uncovered, 30 minutes or until peas are very tender and mixture begins to thicken slightly.

2. Remove from heat and remove ham hocks. Let stand 20 minutes before serving to thicken and allow flavors to blend. Sprinkle with green onions.

OVEN-ROASTED POTATOES AND ONIONS WITH HERBS

Makes 6 servings

3 pounds red potatoes, cut into 1½-inch cubes

1 Vidalia or other sweet onion, coarsely chopped

3 tablespoons olive oil

2 tablespoons butter, melted

3 cloves garlic, minced

¾ teaspoon salt

¾ teaspoon black pepper

⅓ cup packed chopped mixed fresh herbs, such as basil, chives, parsley, oregano, rosemary and/or thyme

1. Preheat oven to 450°F. Line large shallow roasting pan with foil. Arrange potatoes and onion in prepared pan.

2. Combine oil, butter, garlic, salt and pepper in small bowl. Drizzle over potatoes and onion; toss to coat.

3. Bake 30 minutes. Stir; bake 10 minutes. Add herbs; toss well. Bake 10 minutes or until vegetables are tender and browned.

COLLARD GREENS

Makes 10 servings

4 bunches collard greens, stemmed, washed and torn into bite-size pieces

2 cups water

½ medium red bell pepper, cut into strips

⅓ medium green bell pepper, cut into strips

¼ cup olive oil

¼ teaspoon salt

¼ teaspoon black pepper

Place all ingredients in large saucepan; bring to a boil. Reduce heat; simmer 1 to 1½ hours or until tender.

CHEESE SOUFFLÉ

Makes 4 servings

¼ cup (½ stick) butter

¼ cup all-purpose flour

1½ cups milk, at room temperature

¼ teaspoon salt

¼ teaspoon ground red pepper

⅛ teaspoon black pepper

6 eggs, separated

1 cup (4 ounces) shredded Cheddar cheese

Pinch cream of tartar (optional)

1. Preheat oven to 375°F. Grease four 2-cup soufflé dishes or one 2-quart soufflé dish.

2. Melt butter in large saucepan over medium-low heat. Add flour; whisk 2 minutes or until mixture just begins to color. Gradually whisk in milk. Add salt, red pepper and black pepper. Whisk until mixture boils and thickens. Remove from heat. Stir in egg yolks, one at a time, and cheese.

3. Beat egg whites and cream of tartar in large bowl with electric mixer at high speed until stiff peaks form. Gently fold egg whites into cheese mixture until almost combined. (Some streaks of white should remain.) Transfer mixture to prepared dishes.

4. Bake small soufflés about 20 minutes (30 to 40 minutes for large soufflé) or until puffed and browned and skewer inserted into center comes out moist but clean. Serve immediately.

SKILLET SUCCOTASH

Makes 4 servings

1 teaspoon canola oil

½ cup diced onion

½ cup diced green bell pepper

½ cup diced celery

½ teaspoon paprika

¾ cup white or yellow corn

¾ cup lima beans

½ cup canned diced tomatoes

1 tablespoon minced fresh parsley

¼ teaspoon salt

¼ teaspoon black pepper

1. Heat oil in large skillet over medium heat. Add onion, bell pepper and celery; cook and stir 5 minutes or until onion is translucent and vegetables are crisp-tender. Stir in paprika.

2. Add corn, lima beans and tomatoes. Reduce heat; cover and simmer 20 minutes or until beans are tender. Stir in parsley, salt and black pepper just before serving.

TIP: For additional flavor, add 1 clove minced garlic and 1 bay leaf. Remove and discard bay leaf before serving.

SUMMER SQUASH BAKE

Makes 8 servings

- 1 tablespoon vegetable oil
- 1 medium onion, cut into thin wedges
- 1 red bell pepper, cut into thin strips
- 2 yellow squash, quartered and sliced (about 4 cups)
- 1 small zucchini, sliced (about 1½ cups)
- ½ teaspoon salt
- ¼ teaspoon black pepper
- 1 cup (4 ounces) shredded Cheddar cheese
- 1 cup fresh bread crumbs (3 slices bread, crusts removed)
- 1½ tablespoons butter, melted
- ½ teaspoon poultry seasoning

1. Preheat oven to 350°F. Heat oil in 12-inch skillet over medium heat.

2. Add onion and bell pepper; cook and stir 3 minutes. Add squash and zucchini, cook about 6 minutes or until vegetables are crisp-tender, stirring frequently. Stir in salt and pepper.

3. Transfer vegetable mixture to 2-quart baking dish. Top with cheese. Combine bread crumbs, butter and poultry seasoning in small bowl. Sprinkle over cheese.

4. Bake 30 to 35 minutes or until bread crumbs are browned.

KENTUCKY CORNBREAD & SAUSAGE STUFFING

Makes enough stuffing for 5-pound chicken, 8 side-dish servings

- ½ pound BOB EVANS® Original Recipe Roll Sausage
- 3 cups fresh bread cubes, dried or toasted
- 3 cups crumbled prepared cornbread
- 1 large apple, peeled and chopped
- 1 small onion, chopped
- 1 cup chicken or turkey broth
- 2 tablespoons minced fresh parsley
- 1 teaspoon salt
- 1 teaspoon rubbed sage or poultry seasoning
- ¼ teaspoon black pepper

Crumble sausage into small skillet. Cook over medium heat until browned, stirring occasionally. Place sausage and drippings in large bowl. Add remaining ingredients; toss lightly. Use to stuff chicken loosely just before roasting. Or, place stuffing in greased 13×9-inch baking dish. Add additional broth for moister stuffing, if desired. Bake in 350°F oven 30 minutes. Leftover stuffing should be removed from bird and stored separately in refrigerator. Reheat thoroughly before serving.

SERVING SUGGESTION: Double this recipe to stuff 12- to 15-pound turkey.

GREEN BEAN AND EGG SALAD

Makes 6 servings

1 pound green beans, trimmed and cut into 2-inch pieces

3 hard-cooked eggs, peeled and chopped

2 stalks celery, cut into slices

½ cup (2 ounces) Cheddar cheese cubes (¼-inch cubes)

¼ cup chopped red onion

⅓ cup mayonnaise

2 teaspoons cider vinegar

1½ teaspoons sugar

½ teaspoon salt

½ teaspoon celery seed

⅛ teaspoon black pepper

1. Bring large saucepan of salted water to a boil. Add beans; cook 4 minutes or until crisp-tender. Drain and rinse under cold running water.

2. Combine beans, eggs, celery, cheese and onion in large bowl. Combine mayonnaise, vinegar, sugar, salt, celery seed and pepper in small bowl; mix well. Add to bean mixture; mix gently. Toss until all ingredients are coated.

3. Chill at least 1 hour before serving.

BREADS AND BISCUITS

ANADAMA BREAD

2 cups water

½ cup yellow cornmeal

¼ cup (½ stick) butter, cut into ½-inch pieces

½ cup molasses

5½ to 6 cups all-purpose flour, divided

1 package (¼ ounce) active dry yeast

1 teaspoon salt

1. Bring water to a boil in medium saucepan. Whisk in cornmeal; cook 1 minute, whisking constantly. Reduce heat to low; whisk in butter. Cook 3 minutes, stirring frequently. Stir in molasses. Transfer mixture to bowl of stand mixer; let stand 15 to 20 minutes to cool (to about 90°F). Stir in 2 cups flour, yeast and salt on low speed until rough dough forms and cleans sides of mixer bowl.

2. Attach dough hook to mixer. Knead 5 to 7 minutes on low speed, adding remaining flour ½ cup at a time until dough cleans sides of mixer bowl.

3. Shape dough into a ball; place in large greased bowl. Turn dough to grease top. Cover and let rise in warm place about 1 hour or until doubled in size.

4. Punch down dough. Knead dough on well-floured surface 1 minute. Cut dough in half. Cover and let rest 10 minutes.

5. Grease two loaf pans. Shape dough into loaves and place in pans. Cover and let rise in warm place about 30 minutes or until doubled in size.

6. Preheat oven to 350°F. Bake 30 to 35 minutes or until loaves are browned and sound hollow when tapped. Immediately remove from pans; cool on wire racks.

CHEESE-TOPPED HAM BISCUITS

Makes 8 biscuits

- 2 cups biscuit baking mix
- ½ teaspoon crushed dried thyme
- 2 tablespoons cold unsalted butter, thinly sliced
- ⅔ cup milk
- ½ cup finely chopped smoked ham or Canadian bacon

- ¾ cup (3 ounces) shredded Gruyère cheese,* divided
- 2 tablespoons melted butter
- 1 teaspoon Dijon mustard

Gruyère cheese complements flavor of the ham, but you may substitute any cheese, as desired.

1. Preheat oven to 425°F. Line baking sheet with parchment paper or spray with nonstick cooking spray.

2. Combine biscuit mix and thyme in large bowl. Cut in butter with pastry blender or two knives until mixture resembles small coarse crumbs. Gradually stir in milk, adding enough to form a slightly sticky dough. Gently knead in ham and ¼ cup cheese.

3. Turn out dough onto very lightly floured surface. Pat to ¾-inch thickness. Cut out biscuits with 2½-inch biscuit cutter, reworking dough as necessary. Arrange 1 inch apart on prepared baking sheet.

4. Blend melted butter and mustard in small bowl. Brush over each biscuit. Pat 1 tablespoon remaining cheese onto each biscuit.

5. Bake 14 to 17 minutes or until golden brown. Transfer to wire rack to cool.

SWEET POTATO BISCUITS

Makes 12 rolls

1½ cups all-purpose flour

2 tablespoons packed dark brown sugar

1 tablespoon baking powder

½ teaspoon salt

½ teaspoon ground cinnamon

⅛ teaspoon ground nutmeg

5 tablespoons butter, cut into small pieces

1 cold puréed cooked sweet potato (about 1 large sweet potato)

½ cup buttermilk

2 tablespoons honey

1. Preheat oven to 450°F. Spray baking sheet with nonstick cooking spray.

2. Combine 1½ cups flour, brown sugar, baking powder, salt, cinnamon and nutmeg in medium bowl; mix well. Cut in butter with pastry blender or two knives until mixture resembles coarse crumbs. Stir in sweet potato and buttermilk until combined.

3. Transfer dough to floured work surface. Using floured hands, knead dough five times or until no longer sticky, adding additional flour if necessary. Pat dough into ¼-inch thick disc. Cut out dough with 2½-inch round cutter. Reroll scraps and cut out additional pieces. Place 1 inch apart on prepared baking sheet. Refrigerate 20 minutes.

4. Preheat oven to 450°F. Bake 12 to 14 minutes or until biscuits are puffed and light golden brown. Immediately brush tops evenly with honey. Remove to wire rack; cool 5 minutes. Serve warm.

GINGERBREAD PINEAPPLE MUFFINS

Makes 24 muffins

1 can (8 ounces) crushed pineapple in juice, undrained

1 package (14½ ounces) gingerbread cake and cookie mix

¾ cup lukewarm water

1 egg

2 teaspoons canola oil

¼ cup chopped walnuts (optional)

1. Preheat oven to 350°F. Spray 24 mini muffin pan cups with nonstick cooking spray.

2. Place pineapple with juice in fine-mesh sieve over medium bowl; drain well, pressing pineapple to release juices.

3. Combine gingerbread mix, water, pineapple juice, egg and oil in large bowl; whisk 2 minutes, scraping side of bowl often. Stir in walnuts, if desired.

4. Spoon batter into prepared muffin cups. Top each with equal amount of pineapple. Bake 13 to 16 minutes or until toothpick inserted into centers comes out clean. Remove to wire rack; cool completely.

COUNTRY BUTTERMILK BISCUITS

Makes about 9 biscuits

2 cups all-purpose flour

1 tablespoon baking powder

2 teaspoons sugar

½ teaspoon salt

½ teaspoon baking soda

½ cup shortening or cold butter

⅔ cup buttermilk*

Or substitute soured fresh milk. To sour milk, combine 2½ teaspoons lemon juice plus enough milk to equal ⅔ cup. Stir; let stand 5 minutes before using.

1. Preheat oven to 450°F.

2. Combine flour, baking powder, sugar, salt and baking soda in medium bowl. Cut in shortening with pastry blender or two knives until mixture resembles coarse crumbs. Make well in center of dry ingredients. Add buttermilk; stir until mixture forms soft dough that clings together and forms a ball.

3. Turn out dough onto well-floured surface. Knead dough gently 10 to 12 times. Roll or pat dough to ½-inch thickness. Cut out dough with floured 2½-inch biscuit cutter. Place cutouts 2 inches apart on ungreased baking sheet.

4. Bake 8 to 10 minutes or until golden brown. Serve warm.

DROP BISCUITS: Prepare biscuits as directed in step 2, increasing buttermilk to 1 cup. Stir batter with wooden spoon about 15 strokes. *Do not knead.* Drop dough by heaping tablespoonfuls 1 inch apart onto greased baking sheets. Bake as directed in step 4. Makes about 18 biscuits.

SOUR CREAM DILL BISCUITS: Prepare biscuits as directed in step 2, omitting buttermilk. Combine ½ cup sour cream, ⅓ cup milk and 1 tablespoon chopped fresh dill *or* 1 teaspoon dried dill weed in small bowl until well blended. Stir into dry ingredients and continue as directed. Makes about 9 biscuits.

BACON AND ONION BISCUITS: Prepare biscuits as directed in step 2, adding 4 slices crumbled crisp-cooked bacon and ⅓ cup chopped green onions to flour mixture before adding buttermilk. Continue as directed. Makes about 9 biscuits.

BUTTERMILK CORNBREAD

Prep Time: 15 minutes • Cook Time: 25 minutes • Makes 9 servings

REYNOLDS WRAP®
Non-Stick Foil

2 cups buttermilk

2 eggs

¼ cup vegetable oil

2 cups yellow cornmeal

1 teaspoon baking soda

1 teaspoon baking powder

1 teaspoon salt

PREHEAT oven to 450°F. Line an 8-inch square baking pan with REYNOLDS WRAP® Non-Stick Foil; set aside.

STIR together buttermilk, eggs and oil in a large bowl. Add cornmeal, baking soda, baking powder and salt; stir until well blended. Pour batter into foil-lined pan.

BAKE 25 to 30 minutes or until a wooden pick inserted in center comes out clean and cornbread is golden brown.

REYNOLDS KITCHENS TIP: To substitute regular milk for buttermilk, place 1 tablespoon lemon juice or vinegar in a measuring cup. Add enough milk to make 1 cup total liquid. Let stand 5 minutes before using.

HONEY FIG WHOLE WHEAT MUFFINS

Makes 12 muffins

1 cup whole wheat flour

½ cup all-purpose flour

½ cup wheat germ

2 teaspoons baking powder

1 teaspoon ground cinnamon

½ teaspoon salt

½ teaspoon ground nutmeg

½ cup milk

½ cup honey

¼ cup (½ stick) butter, melted

1 egg

1 cup chopped dried figs

½ cup chopped walnuts

1. Preheat oven to 375°F. Grease 12 standard (2½-inch) muffin cups or line with paper baking cups.

2. Combine flours, wheat germ, baking powder, cinnamon, salt and nutmeg in large bowl. Combine milk, honey, butter and egg in small bowl until well blended. Stir into flour mixture just until moistened. Fold in figs and walnuts. Spoon evenly into prepared muffin cups.

3. Bake 20 minutes or until lightly browned on edges and toothpick inserted into center comes out clean. Remove from pan; cool slightly on wire rack.

CINNAMON RAISIN BREAD

Makes 2 loaves

4 cups all-purpose flour

2½ teaspoons salt

2½ teaspoons active dry yeast

¼ cup (½ stick) butter

1 cup plus 2 tablespoons milk

2 tablespoons honey

2 eggs

1 cup raisins

2 tablespoons melted butter, divided

2 tablespoons plus 2 teaspoons sugar

4 teaspoons ground cinnamon

1. Combine flour, salt and yeast in bowl of electric stand mixer. Melt ¼ cup butter in small saucepan over low heat; stir in milk and honey until mixture is warm but not hot. Whisk in eggs; remove from heat.

2. Add egg mixture and raisins to flour mixture. With dough hook, mix on low speed until dough separates from sides of bowl and forms a ball. Continue mixing 2 minutes.

3. Place dough in lightly greased bowl; turn to coat top. Cover loosely with plastic wrap. Let rise in warm place 1 to 1½ hours or until dough is doubled in size.

4. Grease and flour two 8×4-inch loaf pans. Punch down dough and divide in half. Shape each ball into 8×10-inch rectangle. Brush tops of dough with 1 tablespoon melted butter.

5. Combine sugar and cinnamon in small bowl. Reserve 2 teaspoons cinnamon-sugar; sprinkle remaining cinnamon-sugar evenly over dough.

6. Roll up one dough rectangle, starting with short side; place in prepared loaf pan. Repeat with remaining dough. Cover with plastic wrap. Let rise in warm place 1 to 1½ hours or until almost doubled in size. Preheat oven to 375°F.

7. Bake loaves 35 minutes or until golden brown (internal temperature should register 180°F), rotating pans once. Brush tops with remaining 1 tablespoon melted butter; sprinkle with reserved cinnamon-sugar. Cool in pans 10 minutes. Remove to wire rack; cool completely.

SCRUMPTIOUS SANDWICH BREAD

Makes 2 loaves

½ cup milk

3 tablespoons sugar

2 teaspoons salt

3 tablespoons butter

2 packages (¼ ounce each) active dry yeast

1½ cups warm water (105° to 115°F)

5 to 6 cups all-purpose flour

1. Heat milk, sugar, salt and butter in small saucepan over low heat until butter melts and sugar dissolves. Cool to lukewarm (120°F).

2. Dissolve yeast in warm water in bowl of electric mixer. Add milk mixture and 4½ cups flour. Attach dough hook; mix on low speed about 1 minute. Knead on low speed 5 minutes or until dough until dough is smooth, elastic and slightly sticky, adding remaining flour ½ cup at a time.

3. Place dough in greased bowl; turn to grease top. Cover and let rise in warm place about 1 hour or until doubled in size.

4. Grease two 8×4-inch loaf pans. Punch dough down and divide in half. Shape each half into a loaf; place in prepared pans. Cover and let rise in warm place about 1 hour or until doubled in size.

5. Preheat oven to 400°F. Bake 30 minutes or until golden brown. Immediately remove from pans; cool on wire racks.

SIXTY-MINUTE ROLLS: Increase yeast to 3 packages and sugar to ¼ cup; proceed as directed through step 3. Place in greased bowl; turn to grease top. Cover and let rise in warm place about 15 minutes. Turn dough onto lightly floured surface. Shape as desired (see following suggestions). Cover and let rise in slightly warm oven (90°F) about 15 minutes. Preheat oven to 425°F. Bake 12 minutes or until golden brown. Immediately remove from pans; cool on wire racks.

CURLICUES: Divide dough in half and roll each half to 12×9-inch rectangle. Cut 12 equal strips about 1 inch wide. Roll each strip tightly to form a coil, tucking ends underneath. Place on greased baking sheets about 2 inches apart.

CLOVERLEAFS: Divide dough into 24 equal pieces. Form each piece into a ball and place in greased muffin pan. With scissors, cut each ball in half, then quarters.

FARMER-STYLE SOUR CREAM BREAD

Makes 8 to 12 servings

1 cup sour cream, at room temperature

3 tablespoons water

2½ to 3 cups all-purpose flour, divided

1 package (¼ ounce) active dry yeast

2 tablespoons sugar

1½ teaspoons salt

¼ teaspoon baking soda

Vegetable oil

1 tablespoon sesame or poppy seeds

1. Stir together sour cream and water in small saucepan. Heat over low heat until temperature reaches 120° to 130°F. *Do not boil.* Combine 2 cups flour, yeast, sugar, salt and baking soda in large bowl. Stir sour cream mixture into flour mixture until well blended. Turn out dough onto lightly floured surface. Knead about 5 minutes, adding enough remaining flour until dough is smooth and elastic.

2. Grease large baking sheet. Shape dough into a ball; place on prepared baking sheet. Flatten into 8-inch circle. Brush top with oil. Sprinkle with sesame seeds. Invert large bowl over dough and let rise in warm place 1 hour or until doubled in size.

3. Preheat oven to 350°F. Bake 22 to 27 minutes or until golden brown. Immediately remove from baking sheet; cool on wire rack.

GOLD AND WHITE CORNBREAD

Prep Time: 5 minutes • Cook Time: 20 minutes • Total Time: 25 minutes • Makes 12 servings

INGREDIENTS

- 1 cup yellow cornmeal
- 1 cup flour
- ¼ cup sugar
- 1 Tbsp. baking powder
- ½ tsp. salt
- 1 can (15.25 oz.) DEL MONTE® Whole Kernel Gold and White Corn, drained
- 1 can (14.75 oz.) DEL MONTE® Cream Style Corn
- ½ cup (1 stick) butter or margarine, melted
- ¼ cup low-fat milk
- 2 eggs, beaten
- Honey (optional)

DIRECTIONS

1. Preheat oven to 400°F.

2. Combine first 5 ingredients in large bowl; mix well.

3. Combine corn, butter, milk and eggs. Pour into flour mixture; stir just enough to blend.

4. Bake in 8×8-inch square pan for 25 to 30 minutes or pour into 12 large, greased muffin cups for 15 to 20 minutes or until golden brown. Serve with honey.

OATMEAL HONEY BREAD

Makes 1 loaf

1½ to 2 cups all-purpose flour

1 cup plus 1 tablespoon old-fashioned oats, divided

½ cup whole wheat flour

1 package (¼ ounce) rapid-rise active dry yeast

1 teaspoon salt

1⅓ cups plus 1 tablespoon water, divided

¼ cup honey

2 tablespoons butter

1 egg

1. Combine 1½ cups all-purpose flour, 1 cup oats, whole wheat flour, yeast and salt in large bowl.

2. Heat 1⅓ cups water, honey and butter in small saucepan over low heat until honey dissolves and butter melts. Let cool to 130°F. Add to flour mixture; beat with electric mixer at medium speed 2 minutes. Add additional flour by tablespoonfuls until dough begins to cling together. Dough should be shaggy and very sticky, not dry. (Dough will not form a ball and/or clean side of bowl.)

3. Attach dough hook to mixer; knead at medium-low speed 4 minutes. Transfer dough to large greased bowl; turn to grease top. Cover and let rise in warm place 45 minutes or until doubled in size.

4. Spray 8×4-inch loaf pan with nonstick cooking spray. Punch down dough; turn out onto floured work surface. Flatten and stretch dough into 8-inch-long oval. Bring long sides together and pinch to seal; fold over short ends and pinch to seal. Place dough seam side down in prepared pan. Cover and let rise in warm place 20 to 30 minutes or until dough reaches top of pan.

5. Preheat oven to 375°F. Beat egg and remaining 1 tablespoon water in small bowl. Brush top of loaf with some of egg mixture; sprinkle with remaining 1 tablespoon oats.

6. Bake 30 to 35 minutes or until bread sounds hollow when tapped (about 190°F). Cool in pan 10 minutes; remove to wire rack to cool completely.

TIP: To knead by hand, transfer dough to floured work surface. Begin by folding sticky dough over using dough scraper or spatula. When dough becomes more manageable, knead by hand about 6 minutes or until almost smooth. Sprinkle work surface with small amounts of flour as needed to prevent sticking, but dough should remain supple and soft.

CAKES

RED VELVET WHOOPIES

- 1¾ cups all-purpose flour
- ½ teaspoon baking powder
- ½ teaspoon baking soda
- ¼ teaspoon salt
- 2 tablespoons red food coloring
- 1½ tablespoons unsweetened cocoa powder
- 1 cup (2 sticks) butter, softened, divided
- ½ cup granulated sugar
- ½ cup packed brown sugar
- 1 egg
- 2 teaspoons vanilla, divided
- ⅓ cup buttermilk
- 2 teaspoons cider vinegar
- 1 package (8 ounces) cream cheese, softened
- 2½ cups powdered sugar

1. Preheat oven to 350°F. Line three cookie sheets with parchment paper. Combine flour, baking powder, baking soda and salt in medium bowl.

2. Combine food coloring and cocoa powder in large bowl; whisk until smooth paste forms. Add ½ cup butter, granulated sugar and brown sugar; beat with electric mixer at medium speed 3 minutes or until smooth and fluffy. Add egg and 1 teaspoon vanilla; beat 1 minute. Add buttermilk and vinegar; beat 1 minute. Add flour mixture; beat at low speed just until combined. Spoon tablespoonfuls of batter onto prepared cookie sheets.

3. Bake 10 minutes or until tops spring back when lightly touched. Cool on cookie sheets 5 minutes; remove to wire racks to cool completely.

4. For filling, beat cream cheese, remaining ½ cup butter and 1 teaspoon vanilla with electric mixer at medium speed until creamy. Add powdered sugar; beat until creamy and spreadable.

5. Pipe or spread filling onto bottoms of half of cookies; top with remaining cookies.

COCONUT SPICE CAKE

½ cup granulated sugar, plus additional for preparing cake pans

2½ cups all-purpose flour

1½ teaspoons baking powder

¾ teaspoon baking soda

½ teaspoon salt

1½ teaspoons ground cinnamon

¼ teaspoon ground cloves

¼ teaspoon ground nutmeg

¼ teaspoon ground allspice

¼ teaspoon ground cardamom

1½ cups milk

¼ cup molasses

1 teaspoon vanilla

½ cup (1 stick) butter, softened

½ cup packed brown sugar

4 eggs

1½ cups shredded coconut

Creamy Orange Frosting (recipe follows)

Candied Orange Rose (recipe follows, optional)

⅔ cup orange marmalade

1. Preheat oven to 350°F. Spray three (8-inch) round cake pans with nonstick cooking spray. Line bottoms with parchment paper; spray with nonstick cooking spray. Sprinkle with enough granulated sugar to lightly coat bottoms and sides of pans.

2. Combine flour, baking powder, baking soda, salt and spices in medium bowl. Combine milk, molasses and vanilla in small bowl.

3. Beat butter in large bowl with electric mixer at medium speed until creamy. Add ½ cup granulated sugar and brown sugar; beat until light and fluffy. Add eggs, one at a time, beating well after each addition. Add flour mixture alternately with milk mixture, beating well after each addition. Stir in coconut; pour evenly into prepared pans.

4. Bake 20 minutes or until toothpicks inserted into centers come out clean. Cool in pans on wire racks 10 minutes. Loosen edges; turn out onto wire racks. Remove parchment; cool completely.

5. Prepare Creamy Orange Frosting and Candied Orange Rose, if desired.

6. To assemble, spread two cake layers with marmalade; stack on serving plate. Top with third cake layer. Frost with Creamy Orange Frosting and garnish with orange rose. Store in refrigerator.

CREAMY ORANGE FROSTING

3 ounces cream cheese, softened

2 cups powdered sugar

1 teaspoon grated orange peel

4 to 6 teaspoons fresh orange juice

1. Beat cream cheese in large bowl with electric mixer on medium-high speed until creamy.

2. Gradually add powdered sugar on low speed, beating until fluffy. Blend in orange peel and juice, 1 teaspoon at a time, if necessary to reach desired consistency.

CANDIED ORANGE ROSE

1 cup granulated sugar

1 cup water

1 orange

1. Combine sugar and water in medium saucepan. Bring to a boil over high heat, stirring occasionally.

2. Meanwhile, thinly peel orange with sharp knife, leaving as much membrane on orange as possible. Carefully roll up peel, starting at one short end; secure with toothpick. Place on slotted spoon; add to hot sugar syrup.

3. Reduce heat to low; simmer 5 to 10 minutes or until orange rind turns translucent. Remove from syrup; cool on waxed paper.

FRESH BERRY SHORTCAKES WITH WHITE CHOCOLATE MOUSSE

Prep Time: 30 minutes • Chill Time: 1 hour • Bake Time: 15 minutes • Makes 12 servings

WHITE CHOCOLATE MOUSSE

- 6 ounces white chocolate, finely chopped
- 1½ cups heavy cream, divided
- 1 teaspoon SPICE ISLANDS® 100% Pure Bourbon Vanilla Extract

SHORTCAKES

- 2⅓ cups buttermilk baking mix
- ½ cup milk
- 3 tablespoons butter or margarine, melted
- ⅓ cup mini chocolate chips

- ½ teaspoon SPICE ISLANDS® 100% Pure Bourbon Vanilla Extract
- 1 tablespoon sugar
- ½ teaspoon SPICE ISLANDS® Ground Saigon Cinnamon

BERRIES

- 4 cups fresh berries (strawberries, raspberries, blueberries, etc.)
- ¼ cup sugar
- 1 teaspoon SPICE ISLANDS® 100% Pure Bourbon Vanilla Extract

TO MAKE WHITE CHOCOLATE MOUSSE:

STIR white chocolate and ½ cup cream in a heavy saucepan over low heat until chocolate is melted. Transfer chocolate mixture to a large bowl.

COOL until mixture begins to thicken. Beat remaining 1 cup cream with electric mixer until soft peaks form. Gently fold whipped cream and 1 teaspoon vanilla extract into chocolate mixture. Cover and chill at least 1 hour.

TO MAKE SHORTCAKES:

COMBINE baking mix, milk, butter, chocolate chips and ½ teaspoon vanilla until soft dough forms. Drop by 12 spoonfuls onto ungreased baking sheet. Combine 1 tablespoon sugar and cinnamon; sprinkle over shortcakes.

BAKE in preheated 400°F oven for 10 to 12 minutes, or until golden brown. Remove from baking sheet; cool.

TO PREPARE BERRIES:

RINSE and trim berries. Slice if desired. Add ¼ cup sugar and 1 teaspoon vanilla; gently stir. Chill until ready to serve.

TO ASSEMBLE:

SPLIT shortcakes and place each in a shallow bowl. Top with White Chocolate Mousse and berry sauce. Garnish with a fresh mint leaf, if desired.

CREAMY LEMON CHEESECAKE

9 graham crackers, crushed into crumbs

⅓ cup blanched almonds, ground

6 tablespoons (¾ stick) butter, melted

¾ cup plus 2 tablespoons sugar, divided

3 packages (8 ounces each) cream cheese, softened

1 container (15 ounces) ricotta cheese

4 eggs

2 tablespoons finely grated lemon peel

1 teaspoon lemon extract

1 teaspoon vanilla

1. Preheat oven to 375°F.

2. Combine graham cracker crumbs, almonds, butter and 2 tablespoons sugar in small bowl; mix well. Press evenly onto bottom and ½ inch up side of 9-inch springform pan. Bake 5 minutes. Cool on wire rack. *Reduce oven temperature to 325°F.*

3. Beat cream cheese, ricotta cheese, eggs, remaining ¾ cup sugar, lemon peel, lemon extract and vanilla in large bowl with electric mixer at low speed until blended. Beat at high speed 4 to 5 minutes until smooth and creamy. Pour into crust.

4. Bake 1 hour and 10 minutes or until just set in center. *Do not overbake.* Remove to wire rack; cool to room temperature. Cover and refrigerate 4 hours or overnight.

ANGEL FOOD CAKE

Makes 1 (10-inch) tube cake

1¼ cups cake flour, sifted

1⅓ cups plus ½ cup sugar, divided

12 egg whites

1¼ teaspoons cream of tartar

¼ teaspoon salt (optional)

1½ teaspoons vanilla

Fresh strawberries (optional)

1. Preheat oven to 350°F. Sift together flour and ½ cup sugar two times.

2. Beat egg whites with cream of tartar, salt, if desired, and vanilla in large bowl with electric mixer at high speed until soft peaks form.

3. Gradually add remaining 1⅓ cups sugar, beating well after each addition until stiff peaks form. Fold in flour mixture. Pour into *ungreased* 10-inch tube pan.

4. Bake 35 to 40 minutes or until cake springs back when lightly touched.

5. Invert pan; place on top of clean empty bottle. Allow cake to cool completely in pan. Serve with strawberries, if desired.

PRALINE CHEESECAKE

Makes 12 to 16 servings

CHEESECAKE

- 20 whole graham crackers (10 ounces total), broken into 1-inch pieces
- ¾ cup (1½ sticks) unsalted butter, cubed
- 1¾ cups packed dark brown sugar, divided
- 4 packages (8 ounces each) cream cheese, softened
- 3 tablespoons maple syrup
- 3 tablespoons all-purpose flour
- ⅛ teaspoon salt
- 5 eggs
- 2 teaspoons vanilla

TOPPING

- ¾ cup packed dark brown sugar
- ⅓ cup whipping cream
- ¼ cup (½ stick) butter
- 3 tablespoons light corn syrup
- ¼ teaspoon salt
- 3 tablespoons bourbon
- 1½ cups pecan pieces, toasted*

To toast pecans, spread in single layer in heavy-bottomed skillet. Cook over medium heat 1 to 2 minutes, stirring frequently, until nuts are lightly browned. Remove from skillet immediately. Cool before using.

1. Preheat oven to 350°F. Combine graham crackers, butter and ½ cup brown sugar in food processor; pulse until crumbs begin to clump together.* Press crumbs on bottom and up side of 10-inch springform pan. Bake 10 minutes.

2. Beat cream cheese, remaining 1¼ cups brown sugar and maple syrup in large bowl with electric mixer on medium-high speed until smooth. Add flour and ⅛ teaspoon salt; mix well. Add eggs and vanilla; beat until blended, scraping down side of bowl occasionally. Pour batter into crust.

3. Bake 55 to 60 minutes or until edge of cheesecake is puffed and slightly cracked and center is just set. Cool completely in pan on wire rack. Remove side of pan; cover cheesecake with plastic wrap and refrigerate overnight.

4. For topping, combine ¾ cup brown sugar, cream, ¼ cup butter, corn syrup and ¼ teaspoon salt in medium saucepan; bring to a boil over high heat, whisking until sugar dissolves. Reduce heat to medium; boil 1 minute without stirring. Remove from heat. Stir in bourbon, then pecans. Cool completely, stirring occasionally. Cover and refrigerate. To serve, reheat in saucepan over medium heat until warm.

Or place graham crackers in resealable food storage bag and crush with rolling pin. Combine with brown sugar and melted butter. Proceed as directed.

BANANA PUDDING SQUARES

Makes 18 servings

1 cup graham cracker crumbs

2 tablespoons butter, melted

1 package (8 ounces) cream cheese, softened

3 cups milk

2 packages (4-serving size each) banana cream instant pudding and pie filling mix

1 container (8 ounces) whipped topping, divided

2 medium bananas

1. Line 13×9-inch baking pan with foil; spray with nonstick cooking spray.

2. Combine graham cracker crumbs and butter in small bowl; stir until well blended. Press onto bottom of prepared pan.

3. Beat cream cheese in large bowl with electric mixer on low speed until smooth. Add milk and pudding mixes; beat on high speed 2 minutes or until smooth and creamy. Fold in half of whipped topping until well blended. Spread half of pudding mixture over crust.

4. Peel bananas; cut into ¼-inch slices. Arrange bananas evenly over pudding layer. Spoon remaining pudding mixture over bananas; spread remaining whipped topping evenly over pudding mixture.

5. Cover loosely with plastic wrap and refrigerate 2 hours or up to 8 hours.

KING CAKE

CAKE

- 12 ounces (1½ packages) cream cheese, softened
- ½ cup powdered sugar
- ¾ teaspoon vanilla
- 3 tablespoons granulated sugar
- 1½ teaspoons ground cinnamon
- ¼ teaspoon ground nutmeg
- 2 packages (11 ounces each) refrigerated French bread dough
- Plastic baby

ICING

- 1½ cups powdered sugar
- 3 tablespoons whole milk
- Green, yellow and purple decorating sugars

1. Preheat oven to 350°F. Spray large baking sheet with nonstick cooking spray.

2. For filling, beat cream cheese, ½ cup powdered sugar and vanilla in medium bowl with electric mixer on low speed until smooth.

3. Combine granulated sugar, cinnamon and nutmeg in small bowl.

4. Lightly spray work surface with nonstick cooking spray. Unroll one package of dough onto work surface. Unroll second package alongside first, overlapping slightly to make one long piece. Press along seam to seal.

5. Sprinkle cinnamon mixture evenly over dough. Spread cream cheese mixture lengthwise over dough, leaving 1 inch border. Roll up dough, starting with cream cheese side. Pinch along seam to seal in filling. Place dough on prepared baking sheet and gently twist. Attach ends of dough pieces to form large twisted circle (to resemble crown); pinch tightly to seal ends together. Insert plastic baby* underneath dough.

6. Bake 25 to 35 minutes or until golden. *Do not overbake.* Cool completely on baking sheet on wire rack. If filling has leaked, trim away excess while still warm.

7. For icing, combine 1½ cups powdered sugar and milk in 2-cup measuring cup with spout; stir until smooth. Drizzle icing evenly over cake. Sprinkle with decorating sugars, alternating colors to make 3 sections of 3 colors each. Let cake stand at least 1 hour to allow icing to set. Cut into 2- to 3-inch pieces to serve.

Be sure everyone knows there's a plastic baby in the cake. Tradition says the person who gets the baby is king for the day. However, that person also has to provide the next king cake.

PIES AND FRUIT DESSERTS

FIG-STRAWBERRY COBBLER WITH CREAM CHEESE DUMPLINGS

Makes 6 to 8 servings

FILLING

- 1½ pounds fresh strawberries, hulled and quartered
- 1 pound fresh or thawed frozen figs, stemmed and quartered
- ⅓ cup packed brown sugar
- 2 tablespoons cornstarch
- 2 teaspoons grated lemon peel

DUMPLINGS

- 1 cup all-purpose flour
- 1 teaspoon baking powder
- ¼ teaspoon salt
- 1 package (8 ounces) cream cheese or Neufchâtel cheese, softened
- 5 tablespoons granulated sugar, divided
- ½ cup plus 2 tablespoons milk
- 1 teaspoon vanilla

1. Preheat oven to 350°F. Spray 9-inch round or 8-inch square baking dish with nonstick cooking spray.

2. Combine strawberries, figs, brown sugar, cornstarch and lemon peel in medium bowl; toss to coat. Spoon into prepared baking dish.

3. Combine flour, baking powder and salt in medium bowl; mix well. Beat cream cheese and 3 tablespoons granulated sugar in large bowl with electric mixer on high speed until light and fluffy. Add milk and vanilla; beat at medium speed until well blended. Add flour mixture; stir just until moistened. Drop by rounded tablespoonfuls onto fruit mixture; sprinkle with remaining 2 tablespoons granulated sugar.

4. Bake 55 to 60 minutes or until filling is thick and bubbly and dumplings are browned. Let stand 30 minutes before serving.

GINGER PLUM TART

Makes 6 to 8 servings

1 refrigerated pie crust (half of 14-ounce package)

1¾ pounds plums, cut into ½-inch slices

½ cup plus 1 teaspoon sugar, divided

1½ tablespoons all-purpose flour

1½ teaspoons ground ginger

¼ teaspoon ground cinnamon

⅛ teaspoon salt

1 egg

2 teaspoons water

1. Preheat oven to 400°F. Let pie crust stand at room temperature 10 minutes.

2. Combine plums, ½ cup sugar, flour, ginger, cinnamon and salt in large bowl; toss to coat.

3. Roll out crust on lightly floured surface into 14-inch circle. Transfer crust to large (10-inch) ungreased cast iron skillet. Mound plum mixture in center of crust, leaving 2-inch border around fruit. Fold crust up over filling, pleating as necessary and gently pressing crust into fruit to secure.

4. Beat egg and water in small bowl; brush over crust. Sprinkle with remaining 1 teaspoon sugar.

5. Bake about 45 minutes or until crust is golden brown.

COUNTRY PECAN PIE

Makes 8 servings

- 1 refrigerated pie crust (½ of a 15-ounce package)
- 1¼ cups dark corn syrup
- 4 eggs
- ½ cup packed brown sugar
- ¼ cup (½ stick) butter, melted
- 2 teaspoons all-purpose flour
- 1½ teaspoons vanilla
- 1½ cups pecan halves

1. Preheat oven to 350°F. Unroll pastry on lightly floured surface; roll into 13-inch circle. Fit into 9-inch pie plate. Trim and flute edges.

2. Beat corn syrup, eggs, brown sugar and butter in large bowl with electric mixer on medium speed 2 to 3 minutes or until well blended. Stir in flour and vanilla until blended. Pour into pie crust. Arrange pecans on top.

3. Bake 40 to 45 minutes or until center of filling is puffed and golden brown. Cool completely on wire rack.

BLUEBERRY PEACH COBBLER

Makes 8 servings

3 tablespoons butter

4 packages (16 ounces each) frozen sliced peaches, thawed and drained

1 cup fresh blueberries

½ cup packed brown sugar

¼ cup all-purpose flour

½ teaspoon vanilla

¼ teaspoon ground nutmeg

1¼ cups biscuit baking mix

⅓ cup milk

2 tablespoons butter, melted

2 tablespoons granulated sugar

1. Preheat oven to 375°F. Melt 3 tablespoons butter in large skillet (not nonstick) over medium heat. Cook and stir about 3 minutes or until butter has a nutty aroma and turns light brown in color. Add peaches; cook and stir 2 minutes.

2. Combine peaches, blueberries, brown sugar, flour, vanilla and nutmeg in large bowl; toss to coat. Spoon into 2-quart baking dish. Bake 10 minutes.

3. Meanwhile, combine baking mix, milk, 2 tablespoons melted butter and granulated sugar in medium bowl; mix well. Drop eight equal spoonfuls of batter over warm fruit mixture.

4. Bake 30 to 35 minutes or until biscuits are golden brown and cooked on bottom. Cool on wire rack 10 minutes. Serve warm.

APPLE-PEAR PRALINE PIE

Makes 8 servings

Double-Crust Pie Pastry (recipe follows)

4 cups sliced peeled Granny Smith apples

2 cups sliced peeled pears

¾ cup granulated sugar

¼ cup plus 1 tablespoon all-purpose flour, divided

4 teaspoons ground cinnamon

¼ teaspoon salt

½ cup (1 stick) plus 2 tablespoons butter, divided

1 cup packed brown sugar

1 tablespoon half-and-half or milk

1 cup chopped pecans

1. Prepare pie pastry.

2. Combine apples, pears, granulated sugar, ¼ cup flour, cinnamon and salt in large bowl; toss to coat. Let stand 15 minutes.

3. Preheat oven to 350°F. Roll out one disc of pastry into 11-inch circle on floured surface. Line deep-dish 9-inch pie plate with pastry; sprinkle with remaining 1 tablespoon flour. Spoon apple and pear mixture into crust; cube 2 tablespoons butter and scatter over filling. Roll out remaining disc of pastry into 10-inch circle. Place over fruit; seal and flute edge. Cut slits in top crust.

4. Bake 1 hour. Meanwhile, combine remaining ½ cup butter, brown sugar and half-and-half in small saucepan; bring to a boil over medium heat, stirring frequently. Boil 2 minutes, stirring constantly. Remove from heat; stir in pecans. Let stand until slightly thickened. Spread over pie.

5. Cool pie on wire rack 15 minutes. Serve warm or at room temperature.

DOUBLE-CRUST PIE PASTRY: Combine 2½ cups all-purpose flour, 1 teaspoon salt and 1 teaspoon sugar in large bowl. Cut in 1 cup (2 sticks) cubed unsalted butter with pastry blender or electric mixer on low speed until coarse crumbs form. Mix ½ cup ice water and 1 tablespoon cider vinegar in small bowl. Drizzle mixture over flour mixture, 2 tablespoons at a time, stirring just until dough comes together. Divide dough in half. Shape each half into a disc; wrap in plastic wrap. Refrigerate 30 minutes.

BLUEBERRY PIE

Cream Cheese Pastry (recipe follows)

2 pints (4 cups) fresh or thawed frozen blueberries

2 tablespoons cornstarch

⅔ cup blueberry preserves, melted

¼ teaspoon ground nutmeg

1 egg yolk

1 tablespoon sour cream

1. Prepare pastry. Preheat oven to 425°F. Roll out one disc pastry into 11-inch circle on floured surface. Line 9-inch pie plate with pastry.

2. Combine blueberries and cornstarch in medium bowl; toss gently to coat. Add preserves and nutmeg; mix gently. Spoon into crust.

3. Roll out remaining disc pastry into 11-inch circle; place over fruit mixture. Turn edge under and flute. Cut several slits or circle in top crust. If desired, cut leaves from pastry scraps to decorate top of pie.

4. Bake 10 minutes. *Reduce oven temperature to 350°F.* Beat egg yolk and sour cream in small bowl; brush lightly over crust. Bake 40 minutes or until crust is golden brown. Cool 15 minutes on wire rack. Serve warm, at room temperature or chilled.

CREAM CHEESE PASTRY

Makes pastry for one 9-inch pie

1½ cups all-purpose flour

½ cup (1 stick) cold butter

3 ounces cream cheese, cubed

1 teaspoon vanilla

1. Place flour in large bowl. Cut in butter with pastry blender or electric mixer on low speed until mixture resembles coarse crumbs. Cut in cream cheese and vanilla until mixture forms dough.

2. Divide dough in half. Shape each half into a disc; wrap in plastic wrap. Refrigerate 30 minutes.

NOTE: Pastry can be prepared in food processor fitted with steel blade.

STRAWBERRIES 'N' CREAM COBBLER

Makes 6 servings

2 pounds fresh strawberries, hulled and sliced
½ cup strawberry jam
⅔ cup all-purpose flour
⅓ cup sugar
1 teaspoon baking powder
¼ teaspoon salt
2 tablespoons cold butter
¼ cup milk
6 tablespoons whipping cream or melted vanilla ice cream

1. Preheat oven to 375°F. Spray six 8-ounce ramekins or custard cups with nonstick cooking spray.

2. Combine strawberries and jam in large skillet; cook over medium heat about 20 minutes or until thickened and reduced, stirring occasionally.

3. Meanwhile, combine flour, sugar, baking powder and salt in medium bowl; mix well. Cut in butter with pastry blender or electric mixer on low speed until mixture resembles fine crumbs. Stir in milk to make soft dough.

4. Divide strawberry mixture evenly among prepared ramekins. Spoon dough evenly over strawberry mixture, spreading with back of spoon.

5. Bake 20 to 25 minutes or until crust is golden brown. Serve warm; drizzle each cobbler with 1 tablespoon cream.

LEMON TART

Makes 8 to 10 servings

1 refrigerated pie crust (half of 15-ounce package)

5 eggs

1 tablespoon cornstarch

1 cup sugar

½ cup (1 stick) butter

½ cup lemon juice

1. Position rack in center of oven. Preheat oven to 450°F.

2. Line 9-inch tart pan with pie crust, pressing to fit securely against side of pan. Trim off excess crust. Prick bottom and side of crust with fork. Bake 9 to 10 minutes or until golden brown. Cool completely. *Reduce oven temperature to 350°F.*

3. Meanwhile, whisk eggs and cornstarch in medium bowl. Combine sugar, butter and lemon juice in small saucepan; cook and stir over medium-low heat just until butter melts. Whisk in egg mixture; cook 8 to 10 minutes or until thickened, stirring constantly. (Do not let mixture boil.) Pour into medium bowl; stir 1 minute or until cooled slightly. Let cool 10 minutes.

4. Pour cooled lemon curd into baked crust. Bake 25 to 30 minutes or until set. Cool completely before cutting. Store leftovers in refrigerator.

SHOOFLY PIE

Makes 8 servings

1 cup all-purpose flour

⅔ cup packed brown sugar

1 tablespoon cold butter, cut into small pieces

3 eggs, beaten

½ cup molasses

¼ cup (½ stick) butter, melted

½ teaspoon baking soda

⅔ cup hot water

1 unbaked deep-dish 9-inch pie crust

Whipped cream (optional)

1. Preheat oven to 325°F. Combine flour and brown sugar in medium bowl.

2. For topping, remove ½ cup flour mixture to small bowl. Cut in 1 tablespoon cold butter with pastry blender or two knives until mixture resembles coarse crumbs.

3. Whisk eggs, molasses and melted butter in large bowl. Gradually stir in flour mixture until well blended. Stir in baking soda. Gradually stir in hot water until blended. Pour into crust. Sprinkle with topping.

4. Bake 40 minutes or until filling is puffy and set. Cool completely on wire rack. Serve with whipped cream, if desired.

CRUNCH PEACH COBBLER

Makes about 6 to 8 servings

⅓ cup plus 1 tablespoon granulated sugar, divided

1 tablespoon cornstarch

1 can (29 ounces) *or* 2 cans (16 ounces each) cling peach slices in juice, drained and ¾ cup juice reserved

½ teaspoon vanilla

2 cups all-purpose flour, divided

½ cup packed brown sugar

⅓ cup old-fashioned or quick oats

¼ cup (½ stick) butter, melted

½ teaspoon ground cinnamon

½ teaspoon salt

½ cup shortening or cold butter

4 to 5 tablespoons cold water

Whipped cream (optional)

1. Combine ⅓ cup granulated sugar and cornstarch in small saucepan. Slowly add reserved ¾ cup peach juice; mix well. Cook over low heat until thickened, stirring constantly. Remove from heat; stir in vanilla.

2. Combine ½ cup flour, brown sugar, oats, butter and cinnamon in small bowl; stir until mixture forms coarse crumbs. Set aside.

3. Preheat oven to 350°F. Combine remaining 1½ cups flour, 1 tablespoon granulated sugar and salt in medium bowl; mix well. Cut in shortening with pastry blender or two knives until mixture resembles coarse crumbs. Sprinkle water, 1 tablespoon at a time, over flour mixture. Toss lightly with fork after each addition until mixture holds together. Press together to form a ball.

4. Roll out dough into 10-inch square, ⅛-inch thick. Press dough onto bottom and about 1 inch up sides of 8-inch square baking dish. Arrange peaches over crust; pour peach sauce over peaches. Sprinkle with crumb topping.

5. Bake 45 minutes or until topping is golden brown. Serve warm or at room temperature with whipped cream, if desired.

STRAWBERRY RHUBARB PIE

Makes 8 servings

Double-Crust Pie Pastry (page 160)
1½ cups sugar
½ cup cornstarch
2 tablespoons quick-cooking tapioca
1 tablespoon grated lemon peel

¼ teaspoon ground allspice
4 cups sliced rhubarb (1-inch pieces)
3 cups sliced fresh strawberries
1 egg, lightly beaten

1. Prepare pie pastry. Preheat oven to 425°F. Roll out one pastry disc into 11-inch circle on floured surface. Line 9-inch pie plate with pastry.

2. Combine sugar, cornstarch, tapioca, lemon peel and allspice in large bowl. Add rhubarb and strawberries; toss to coat. Pour into crust.

3. Roll out remaining pastry disc into 10-inch circle; cut into ½-inch-wide strips. Arrange in lattice design over fruit. Seal and flute edge. Brush pastry with beaten egg.

4. Bake 50 minutes or until filling is thick and bubbly and crust is golden brown. Cool on wire rack. Serve warm or at room temperature.

COOKIES AND CANDIES

CHOCOLATE-COCONUT-TOFFEE DELIGHTS

Makes 1 dozen large cookies

½ cup all-purpose flour

¼ teaspoon baking powder

¼ teaspoon salt

1 package (12 ounces) semisweet chocolate chips, divided

¼ cup butter (½ stick), cut into small pieces

¾ cup packed brown sugar

2 eggs, beaten

1 teaspoon vanilla

1½ cups flaked coconut

1 cup toffee baking bits

½ cup bittersweet chocolate chips

1. Preheat oven to 350°F. Line cookie sheets with parchment paper. Combine flour, baking powder and salt in small bowl.

2. Place 1 cup semisweet chocolate chips and butter in large microwavable bowl. Microwave on HIGH 1 minute; stir. Microwave at additional 30-second intervals, stirring after each interval, until mixture is melted and smooth.

3. Beat brown sugar, eggs and vanilla with electric mixer on medium speed until well blended. Beat in chocolate mixture until well blended. Add flour mixture; beat at low speed until blended. Stir in coconut, toffee bits and remaining 1 cup semisweet chocolate chips. Drop dough by heaping ⅓ cupfuls 3 inches apart onto prepared cookie sheets. Flatten with rubber spatula into 3½-inch circles.

4. Bake 15 to 17 minutes or until edges are firm. Cool on cookie sheets 2 minutes; slide parchment paper and cookies onto wire racks. Cool completely.

5. For chocolate drizzle, place bittersweet chocolate chips in small microwavable bowl. Microwave on HIGH 30 seconds; stir. Microwave at additional 30-second intervals, stirring after each interval, until melted and smooth. Drizzle over cookies using fork. Let stand until set.

NEW ORLEANS-STYLE PRALINES

Makes about 34 pralines (1¼ pounds)

2 cups packed light brown sugar

1 cup half-and-half

¼ teaspoon salt

2 tablespoons butter

2 tablespoons bourbon or cognac

1½ cups pecan halves

1. Line two baking sheets with foil. Combine brown sugar, half-and-half and salt in heavy 2-quart saucepan. Cook over medium heat until sugar is dissolved and mixture begins to boil, stirring occasionally.

2. Attach candy thermometer to side of pan, making sure bulb is submerged in sugar mixture but not touching bottom of pan. Continue boiling about 20 minutes or until sugar mixture reaches soft-ball stage (235° to 240°F) on candy thermometer, stirring occasionally. (Watch carefully because candy will be grainy if overcooked.) Remove from heat; stir in butter and bourbon. Stir in pecans.

3. Beat with wooden spoon 3 to 4 minutes until temperature drops to 155°F on candy thermometer and mixture is thickened and glossy. Quickly drop mixture by tablespoonfuls onto prepared baking sheets. (If mixture becomes too thick, stir in 1 to 2 teaspoons hot water and reheat over medium heat until mixture reaches 155°F on candy thermometer.) Cool completely. Store in airtight container at room temperature up to 3 days.

NO-BAKE BON BON COOKIES

Makes about 6 dozen cookies

3½ cups vanilla wafers, crushed into fine crumbs

1 cup chopped walnuts

1 cup powdered sugar

⅓ cup peach-flavored bourbon

¼ cup light corn syrup

2 tablespoons unsweetened cocoa powder

6 ounces semisweet chocolate chips

1 tablespoon butter

1. Line cookie sheets with waxed paper.

2. Combine vanilla wafer crumbs, walnuts, powdered sugar, bourbon, corn syrup and cocoa in large bowl; beat by hand until well blended. (Mixture will be very thick and dense.)

3. Shape tablespoonfuls of mixture into balls; place on prepared cookie sheets.

4. Melt chocolate chips and butter in medium saucepan over low heat. Dip balls in chocolate mixture to coat; return to cookie sheets. Refrigerate overnight. Serve cold.

FROSTED SUGAR COOKIES

Makes 7 dozen cookies

2 cups all-purpose flour	2 egg whites
1 teaspoon baking powder	1 teaspoon vanilla
½ teaspoon salt	Vanilla Frosting (recipe follows)
1 cup granulated sugar	Decors and sprinkles
10 tablespoons butter, softened	

1. Preheat oven to 375°F. Line cookie sheets with parchment. Combine flour, baking powder and salt in medium bowl.

2. Beat granulated sugar and butter in large bowl with electric mixer at medium speed until fluffy. Beat in egg whites and vanilla. Add flour mixture; mix well. Wrap in plastic wrap; refrigerate 3 to 4 hours or until firm.

3. Roll out dough on generously floured surface to ¼-inch thickness. (Dough will be soft.) Cut dough into shapes with 2-inch cookie cutters; place on prepared cookie sheets.

4. Bake 8 to 10 minutes or until golden brown. Remove from cookie sheets to wire racks; cool completely. Meanwhile, prepare Vanilla Frosting.

5. Frost cookies; decorate as desired.

VANILLA FROSTING

Makes about ½ cup frosting

2 cups powdered sugar	1 teaspoon vanilla
2 to 3 tablespoons milk, divided	

Whisk powdered sugar, 2 tablespoons milk and vanilla in medium bowl. Add additional 1 tablespoon milk, if necessary, until desired spreading consistency is reached.

HERMITS

Makes about 4 dozen cookies

- 6 tablespoons (¾ stick) butter, softened
- ¼ cup packed dark brown sugar
- 1 egg
- 1 package (about 15 ounces) yellow cake mix
- ⅓ cup molasses
- 1 teaspoon ground cinnamon
- ¼ teaspoon baking soda
- ¾ cup raisins
- ¾ cup chopped pecans
- 2 tablespoons plus 1½ teaspoons maple syrup
- 1 tablespoon butter, melted
- ¼ teaspoon maple flavoring
- ¾ cup powdered sugar

1. Preheat oven to 375°F. Line cookie sheets with parchment paper.

2. Beat softened butter and brown sugar in large bowl with electric mixer on medium speed until well blended. Beat in egg. Add cake mix, molasses, cinnamon and baking soda; beat just until blended. Stir in raisins and pecans. Drop dough by rounded tablespoonfuls about 2 inches apart onto prepared cookie sheets.

3. Bake 13 to 15 minutes or until set. Cool on cookie sheets 5 minutes. Remove to wire racks; cool completely.

4. Combine maple syrup, melted butter and maple flavoring in medium bowl. Add powdered sugar, ¼ cup at a time, stirring until smooth. Spread glaze over cookies; let stand 30 minutes or until set.

DIVINITY

Makes about 40 pieces

½ cup corn syrup
½ cup water
2¼ cups sugar
2 egg whites

⅛ teaspoon cream of tartar
1 teaspoon vanilla
½ cup chopped almonds (optional)

1. Line several baking sheets with waxed paper; grease paper.

2. Combine corn syrup, water and sugar in heavy medium saucepan. Cook over medium heat until sugar dissolves and mixture comes to a boil, stirring constantly. Wash down side of pan frequently with pastry brush dipped in hot water to remove sugar crystals. Clip candy thermometer to side of saucepan, making sure bulb is submerged in sugar mixture but not touching bottom of pan. Continue to cook until mixture reaches 255°F (hard-ball stage).

3. Meanwhile, beat egg whites and cream of tartar in large bowl with electric mixer on high speed until stiff but not dry. With mixer running, pour in hot syrup in thin steady stream. Add vanilla; beat until candy forms soft peaks and starts to lose its gloss. Stir in almonds, if desired. Immediately drop tablespoonfuls of candy into mounds on prepared baking sheets.

4. Store in airtight container in refrigerator between layers of waxed paper or freeze up to 3 months.

HONEY GINGERSNAPS

Makes 3½ dozen cookies

2 **cups all-purpose flour**	¼ **cup (½ stick) butter, softened**
1 **tablespoon ground ginger**	1½ **cups sugar, divided**
2 **teaspoons baking soda**	¼ **cup honey**
⅛ **teaspoon salt**	1 **egg**
⅛ **teaspoon ground cloves**	1 **teaspoon vanilla**
½ **cup shortening**	

1. Preheat oven to 350°F. Line cookie sheets with parchment paper or spray with nonstick cooking spray. Combine flour, ginger, baking soda, salt and cloves in medium bowl.

2. Beat shortening and butter in large bowl with electric mixer on medium speed until smooth. Gradually beat in 1 cup sugar until blended; increase speed to high and beat until light and fluffy. Beat in honey, egg and vanilla until fluffy. Gradually stir in flour mixture until blended.

3. Shape dough into 1-inch balls. Place remaining ½ cup sugar in shallow bowl; roll balls in sugar to coat. Place 2 inches apart on prepared cookie sheets.

4. Bake 10 minutes or until golden brown. Cool on cookie sheets 5 minutes. Remove to wire racks; cool completely. Store in airtight container up to 1 week.

BANANA SANDIES

Makes about 2 dozen sandwich cookies

2⅓ cups all-purpose flour

1 cup (2 sticks) butter, softened

¾ cup granulated sugar

¼ cup packed brown sugar

1 medium banana, cut into ¼-inch slices (about ½ cup)

1 teaspoon vanilla

¼ teaspoon salt

⅔ cup chopped pecans

Prepared cream cheese frosting

Yellow food coloring (optional)

1. Preheat oven to 350°F. Grease cookie sheets.

2. Combine flour, butter, sugars, banana, vanilla and salt in large bowl. Beat 2 to 3 minutes, with electric mixer on medium speed until well blended. Stir in pecans. Shape dough into 1-inch balls. Place 2 inches apart on prepared cookie sheets; flatten to ¼-inch thickness with bottom of glass dipped in sugar.

3. Bake 12 to 15 minutes or until edges are lightly browned. Remove immediately to wire racks; cool completely.

4. Tint frosting with food coloring, if desired. Pipe or spread 1 tablespoon frosting over bottom halves of cookies. Top with remaining cookies.

SNICKERDOODLES

¾ cup plus 2 tablespoons
   sugar, divided

2 teaspoons ground cinnamon,
   divided

1⅓ cups all-purpose flour

1 teaspoon cream of tartar

½ teaspoon baking soda

½ teaspoon salt

½ cup (1 stick) butter, softened

1 egg

1. Preheat oven to 375°F. Line cookie sheet with parchment paper. Combine 2 tablespoons sugar and 1 teaspoon cinnamon in small bowl.

2. Combine flour, remaining 1 teaspoon cinnamon, cream of tartar, baking soda and salt in medium bowl.

3. Beat remaining ¾ cup sugar and butter in large bowl with electric mixer on medium speed until creamy. Beat in egg. Gradually add flour mixture, beating on low speed until stiff dough forms. Roll dough into 1-inch balls; roll in cinnamon-sugar mixture. Place on prepared cookie sheets.

4. Bake 10 minutes or until set. *Do not overbake.* Remove to wire racks; cool completely.

FUDGY MARSHMALLOW POPCORN

Makes about 4 quarts popcorn

3½ quarts popped popcorn

2 cups sugar

1 cup evaporated milk

¼ cup (½ stick) butter

1 cup (½ of 7-ounce jar) marshmallow creme

1 cup (6 ounces) semisweet chocolate chips

1 teaspoon vanilla

1. Place popcorn in large bowl; set aside. Spray baking sheets with nonstick cooking spray or line with parchment paper.

2. Combine sugar, evaporated milk and butter in medium saucepan. Cook over medium heat until sugar is dissolved and mixture comes to a boil, stirring constantly. Boil 5 minutes. Remove from heat.

3. Stir in marshmallow creme, chocolate chips and vanilla until chocolate is melted and mixture is smooth. Pour over popcorn, stirring until completely coated. Spread in single layer on prepared baking sheets. Refrigerate until set.

HINT: Remove any unpopped kernels before measuring the popped popcorn.

PUMPKIN SEED BRITTLE

Makes about 2 pounds brittle

2 cups sugar

1 cup water

1 cup corn syrup

¼ teaspoon cream of tartar

¼ teaspoon salt

2 cups roasted salted pumpkin seeds (pepitas)

1 tablespoon butter, cut into small pieces

½ teaspoon baking soda

1. Grease two baking sheets.

2. Combine sugar, water, corn syrup, cream of tartar and salt in heavy medium saucepan; cook over medium heat until sugar dissolves and mixture boils, stirring constantly. Wash down side of saucepan with pastry brush dipped in hot water to remove sugar crystals.

3. Clip candy thermometer to side of saucepan, making sure bulb is submerged in sugar mixture but not touching bottom of pan. Continue to cook until mixture reaches 238°F (soft-ball stage). Stir in pumpkin seeds; cook until mixture reaches 295°F.

4. Remove from heat; stir in butter and baking soda. Immediately pour hot mixture onto prepared baking sheets. Working quickly, use two forks to stretch mixture as thin as possible. Let stand until set. Break into pieces. Store in airtight container.

FIGGY TARTS

Makes 4 dozen tarts

- ¾ cup (1½ sticks) butter, softened
- ¾ cup granulated sugar
- 3 egg yolks
- 1 teaspoon vanilla
- 2 cups all-purpose flour
- ¼ teaspoon salt
- 1½ cups chopped dried figs

- ½ cup orange juice
- ¼ cup light corn syrup
- 2 tablespoons packed brown sugar
- 2 tablespoons grated orange peel
- ¼ teaspoon ground cinnamon
- Pinch ground cloves

1. Beat butter and granulated sugar in large bowl with electric mixer at medium speed 1 minute. Beat in egg yolks and vanilla until well blended. Add flour and salt; beat just until combined. Shape dough into two discs; wrap in plastic wrap. Refrigerate 1 hour or until firm.

2. Meanwhile for filling, combine figs, juice, corn syrup, brown sugar, orange peel, cinnamon and cloves in medium saucepan. Cook and stir over low heat 5 minutes or until figs are softened. Set aside to cool.

3. Spray 48 mini (1¾-inch) muffin cups with nonstick cooking spray. Roll out half of dough to ⅛-inch thickness on lightly floured surface. Cut out circles with 2½-inch fluted round cookie cutter. Place in prepared muffin cups, pressing dough onto bottoms and up sides of cups and sealing any cracks. Repeat with remaining dough. Reroll dough scraps once. Refrigerate at least 30 minutes before baking.

4. Preheat oven to 375°F. Prick holes in bottom of each tart shell with fork. Bake 10 to 12 minutes or until golden brown. Cool in pans on wire racks 10 minutes.

5. Spoon about 1 tablespoon filling into each crust; refrigerate until ready to serve.

PEANUT BUTTER FUDGE

Makes about 1¼ pounds fudge

1½ cups granulated sugar

1½ cups packed brown sugar

½ cup milk

1 tablespoon unsweetened cocoa powder

1 cup creamy or chunky peanut butter

½ cup (1 stick) butter

1 teaspoon vanilla

1. Grease 13×9-inch pan (or 9-inch square pan for thicker fudge). Combine granulated sugar, brown sugar, milk and cocoa in large saucepan. Clip candy thermometer to side of saucepan, making sure bulb is submerged in sugar mixture but not touching bottom of pan. Cook over medium heat to 238°F (soft-ball stage), stirring constantly.

2. Remove from heat. Add peanut butter, butter and vanilla; stir until melted. Pour into prepared pan. Cool completely. Cut into 1-inch squares.

TIP: For easy clean-up, line pan with foil, leaving 1-inch overhang on sides, and grease foil. Lift cooled fudge out of pan and cut into squares.

ACKNOWLEDGMENTS

The publisher would like to thank the companies listed below for the use of their recipes and photographs in this publication:

ACH Food Companies, Inc.

Bob Evans®

Cream of Wheat® Cereal, A Division
of B&G Foods North America, Inc.

Del Monte Foods

Dole Food Company, Inc.

Jennie-O Turkey Store, LLC

Ortega®, A Division of B&G Foods
North America, Inc.

Pinnacle Foods

Recipes courtesy of the Reynolds
Kitchens

Unilever

METRIC CONVERSION CHART

VOLUME MEASUREMENTS (dry)

$\frac{1}{8}$ teaspoon = 0.5 mL
$\frac{1}{4}$ teaspoon = 1 mL
$\frac{1}{2}$ teaspoon = 2 mL
$\frac{3}{4}$ teaspoon = 4 mL
1 teaspoon = 5 mL
1 tablespoon = 15 mL
2 tablespoons = 30 mL
$\frac{1}{4}$ cup = 60 mL
$\frac{1}{3}$ cup = 75 mL
$\frac{1}{2}$ cup = 125 mL
$\frac{2}{3}$ cup = 150 mL
$\frac{3}{4}$ cup = 175 mL
1 cup = 250 mL
2 cups = 1 pint = 500 mL
3 cups = 750 mL
4 cups = 1 quart = 1 L

VOLUME MEASUREMENTS (fluid)

1 fluid ounce (2 tablespoons) = 30 mL
4 fluid ounces ($\frac{1}{2}$ cup) = 125 mL
8 fluid ounces (1 cup) = 250 mL
12 fluid ounces (1$\frac{1}{2}$ cups) = 375 mL
16 fluid ounces (2 cups) = 500 mL

WEIGHTS (mass)

$\frac{1}{2}$ ounce = 15 g
1 ounce = 30 g
3 ounces = 90 g
4 ounces = 120 g
8 ounces = 225 g
10 ounces = 285 g
12 ounces = 360 g
16 ounces = 1 pound = 450 g

DIMENSIONS

$\frac{1}{16}$ inch = 2 mm
$\frac{1}{8}$ inch = 3 mm
$\frac{1}{4}$ inch = 6 mm
$\frac{1}{2}$ inch = 1.5 cm
$\frac{3}{4}$ inch = 2 cm
1 inch = 2.5 cm

OVEN TEMPERATURES

250°F = 120°C
275°F = 140°C
300°F = 150°C
325°F = 160°C
350°F = 180°C
375°F = 190°C
400°F = 200°C
425°F = 220°C
450°F = 230°C

BAKING PAN SIZES

Utensil	Size in Inches/Quarts	Metric Volume	Size in Centimeters
Baking or Cake Pan (square or rectangular)	8×8×2	2 L	20×20×5
	9×9×2	2.5 L	23×23×5
	12×8×2	3 L	30×20×5
	13×9×2	3.5 L	33×23×5
Loaf Pan	8×4×3	1.5 L	20×10×7
	9×5×3	2 L	23×13×7
Round Layer Cake Pan	8×1½	1.2 L	20×4
	9×1½	1.5 L	23×4
Pie Plate	8×1¼	750 mL	20×3
	9×1¼	1 L	23×3
Baking Dish or Casserole	1 quart	1 L	—
	1½ quart	1.5 L	—
	2 quart	2 L	—